Sunday Times Bestselling Author

DAN TOOMBS

THE CURRY GUY SLOW COOKER

50 Simple Curry Favourites

Photography by Kris Kirkham

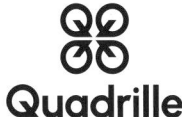

Quadrille

For Edie

CONTENTS

PREFACE

The best curries, stews and soups are those that are slowly cooked for hours. There's something magical about a pot of curry simmering away – the aroma of toasted spices, the rich swirl of coconut milk, the slow melding of garlic, ginger and chillies... That is what made me want to write this book. In our fast-paced lives, many of us don't have the time to hover over a bubbling pot, and that's where the slow cooker becomes a game-changer.

In this book you will find all the most popular curry house-style curries, authentic Indian and Pakistani curries and some reworked classics from South East Asia. You will also find other traditional recipes – such as Lamb Raan (page 62) and Tandoori Chicken (page 61) – which you may never have thought of trying to make in a slow cooker but which, with a few additional steps, work exceptionally well.

In addition to the delicious main courses, I've also included easy homemade curry pastes and spice blends, a simple guide to the most essential ingredients, tips on preparing ahead and advice on adjusting the balance of flavours in your recipes.

With this cookbook I'm not trying to replace time-honoured cooking techniques. Instead, I'm hoping to make traditional recipes more everyday. Whether you're a busy parent, a student in a small kitchen, or simply someone who loves a good, easy meal, the recipes here are designed to give you authentic taste with minimal fuss.

At first glance, using a slow cooker for a cuisine known for fast stir-frying and spice tempering might seem like a mismatch. But slow cookers are perfectly suited to the rich, layered cooking styles of South East Asia and the Indian subcontinent. They're even great for dishes that aren't traditionally slow cooked, such as British curry house style curries.

These cuisines all benefit from cooking meats slowly for depth of flavour and the gradual release of the aromatics. What's more, you can take steps to make the dishes look and taste just as if they were cooked in more traditional methods. All is explained.

Whether it's a Malaysian beef rendang or a classic North Indian butter chicken, slow cooking allows the ingredients to melt into one another, often with less fuss and more flexibility than stovetop methods. It's also easy to try the finished dish, then adjust the texture to your preference. Quick fixes are no problem!

Some of you will have this book in your hands because you want ease of cooking, others are looking for superior results – and most of you are somewhere in between. For this reason, I have given the recipes exactly as I make them at home. Searing meats, paneer, seafood and vegetables before slow cooking adds a lot of flavour so that is what I advise. The recipes are simply better with these additional steps but if you're looking for fuss-free cooking, you could always just throw the ingredients in your slow cooker – you will still end up with a tasty dish. The choice is yours. These are recipes that you can tailor to your lifestyle.

So let's get cooking! This book is for anyone who loves to explore the world through food – for people who want dinner to be effortless but not boring, and who believe that a slow cooker can do more than make soup. You will be amazed at what comes out of your slow cooker!

I hope you enjoy cooking these recipes as much as I enjoyed developing them. As always, if you have any recipe questions, please get in touch. I am @TheCurryGuy on X, Facebook and Instagram and I'm always happy to help.

Happy Cooking!
Dan

LET'S GET STARTED

ABOUT THE RECIPES

Many of you will already have a slow cooker and will know how tasty the results can be, but if you are new to this way of cooking, you are in for a real treat.

Food has been slow cooked for thousands of years but the modern slow cooker is one of the easiest and most convenient ways to slow cook. In addition, they are also economical – it only costs pennies per hour to cook your meal. What's more, it's the cheaper cuts of meat that work best in a slow cooker, becoming out-of-this-world tender, so you will be enjoying amazing flavours at a fraction of the cost of faster cooking methods.

COOKING TIMES

Please treat the cooking times as guides and not gospel. Cooking times can, and probably will, vary depending on your cooker and ingredients. You may find that your curry is ready before the stated time but, remember, this is slow cooking! Letting the curry stew a little longer adds more depth of flavour.

I recommend paying close attention to your first few cooks and getting to know your slow cooker if you don't already. I have found that lamb leg meat in a curry is deliciously tender after about three hours on high. Shoulder and neck can take up to four hours. Chicken breast meat cooks faster than thigh meat but can become stringy if cooked too long, so keep experimenting.

HOW SLOW COOKERS WORK

Slow cookers use a heating element at the base which gradually transfers heat to a ceramic or metal cooking pot. The heat is evenly distributed, allowing you to cook food slowly and consistently.

Most slow cookers come with three settings: low, high and keep warm. The low setting is used to cook food for between six and ten hours and sometimes longer. The high setting gets it all cooked in three to six hours. Using the keep warm feature, you can safely maintain the perfect temperature before serving, without overcooking. Some advanced models will automatically switch to keep warm after the cook is finished. Some models also have a sauté/searing option; if you don't have one, all the recipes tell you how to use a pan instead.

WHICH SIZE SLOW COOKER IS BEST?

Slow cookers come in a variety of sizes and you can cook most – but not all – the recipes in this book with even the smallest of cookers. I prefer larger cookers: they are great for batch cooking and cooking roasts but you should choose the size that best meets your requirements.

- 1.5–3 litres (1.5–3 quarts): Ideal for singles and couples but has limited space if you want to entertain friends.
- 4–6 litres (4–6 quarts): Great for families of four to six people.
- 7–8 litres (7–8.5 quarts): This is the size I use most. Larger models are ideal for families and batch cooking broths, as well as larger joints of meat like the Tandoori chicken (page 61). If you have limited counter space, you might find this too big.

TIPS FOR SUCCESS

Get to know your slow cooker: You will be able to prepare most of the recipes in this book with whichever cooker you have. Different brands cook differently so getting to know your cooker will help you adjust cooking times accordingly. Remember to use your eyes and intuition until you really get to know how your cooker works.

Consider upgrading your slow cooker:
If you are using an older slow cooker, you might want to consider upgrading to a new model or a multi-cooker. Multi-cookers have many more functions – such as searing, braising, baking, steaming and air frying – that will make cooking these and other recipes even easier.

Fry and sear: Although you can simply add all the ingredients to your slow cooker, you will get superior results if you fry and sear the meat and aromatics like garlic, ginger and onion first. When you have a little extra time, the additional effort is worth it, as it is a real flavour booster.

Don't add too much liquid: Using your eyes and intuition is good when cooking but don't be fooled. Many people think that more liquid needs to be added when they look at all the ingredients in the slow cooker. When you slow cook, almost all the ingredients in the pot will release more moisture. If you add more liquid than called for, it will not reduce down over the low cooking heat and your meal could become too watery. These recipes are really easy to get right though! At the end of cooking, you can cook the liquids down to thicken, or add a drop more stock or other liquid to thin.

Choose cheaper cuts of meat: You can and should remove any excess surface fat and chicken skin, but cheaper, fattier cuts hold their shape better and become much more tender and delicious than more expensive cuts, such as chicken breast or pork tenderloin, which tend to dry out when slow cooked. If you do opt for these cuts, you might need to cook for less time.

Use the best-quality ingredients: Fresher ingredients give better flavour. If you do need to use frozen meat or seafood, be sure to defrost it completely first before adding it to your cooker.

INGREDIENTS

I always have the following ingredients on hand because they can be used in so many of the recipes.

WET INGREDIENTS
- Light soy sauce
- Dark soy sauce
- Kecap manis (sweet syrupy soy sauce)
- Oyster sauce
- Shrimp paste
- Thai fish sauce
- Distilled white vinegar
- White wine vinegar

DRY INGREDIENTS
- Rice noodles
- Instant ramen noodles
- Dried Chinese egg noodles
- Palm sugar
- Chapati flour
- Chana lentils
- Masoor lentils
- Black urad lentils
- Coconut milk powder or coconut flour
- Dried chickpeas (garbanzos)
- Dried kidney beans
- Dried Kashmiri chillies
- Cashews
- Candlenuts

WHOLE SPICES AND SPICE BLENDS
You will get a better flavour if you prepare your own spice blends using whole spices, but you can absolutely purchase them if you prefer. Whole or ground, I recommend you do as I do and buy from Asian grocers, as you will get a lot more for your money.

When time permits, I roast and grind all my spices from whole just as I do when I prepare spice blends, so, if you like, you could toast cumin seeds in the same way and grind your

your own homemade ground cumin, for example. You will get a better flavour. I always keep the following whole spices and ground spices/spice blends in
my cupboard:

- Mixed powder (page 118)
- Garam masala (page 119)
- Tandoori masala (page 119)
- Kashmiri chilli powder
- Black peppercorns
- Green cardamom pods
- Ground cumin and/or cumin seeds
- Ground coriander and/or coriander seeds
- Fennel seeds
- Cloves
- Real or Ceylon cinnamon sticks
- (see page 20)
- Ground turmeric
- Amchoor (dried mango powder)
- Kasoori methi (dried fenugreek leaves)

TINNED AND PACKAGED INGREDIENTS
- Shrimp paste
- Passata
- Tinned (canned) chopped tomatoes
- Thick coconut milk
- Chickpeas (gawrbanzos)
- Kidney beans

FRESH AND FROZEN INGREDIENTS
Garlic, galangal, ginger, chillies, curry leaves and tofu can all be frozen. Herbs can also be frozen to use in curries and stocks but will not make an attractive garnish if defrosted.

- Garlic
- Galangal
- Ginger
- Garlic and ginger paste
- Red and green finger chillies
- Red spur chillies
- Coriander (cilantro)
- Mint leaves
- Firm tofu (a good vegan and vegetarian
- protein substitute)
- Paneer (a good vegetarian protein
- substitute)

OILS
I use rapeseed (canola) oil, coconut oil and ghee in my curries because they can be cooked over a high heat, which is perfect for curries. You can use any neutral oil you like that has a high smoking point. So if you prefer sunflower, avocado or any other oil that can take high temperatures, use that. Just don't use olive oil. It tastes great on a salad but it can't take the high heat required for most curries.

CURRY HOUSE STYLE CURRIES

I want to make a few things very clear before you try these recipes – there are rules that you need to follow if you want spectacular results. Stick to the principles on the following pages and you could even surprise yourself as to just how delicious these recipes can be.

SEARING MAKES PERFECT

If all you want is a good easy curry, you could just add all the ingredients, stir and slow cook. The only exception to this is when a curry calls for cream or yogurt, both of which are best added at the end of cooking and heated through just before serving. I have developed the recipes for optimum flavour and sauce consistency, so to make the recipes as written, you will need to take a few additional steps – such as searing, frying and blending – but it's worth the effort and not at all difficult.

ADJUSTING FLAVOURS

The most important part of cooking is getting the flavour right for your personal tastes. I wrote these recipes the way I like them but feel free to adjust the spicing as you see fit. Want more chilli powder? Go for it. Not crazy about cumin? Leave it out. Taste as you cook and adjust. I have kept things simple in the recipes but if you would like to add even more amazing flavour, try marinating your meat, poultry, paneer, seafood or vegetables in my easy tandoori marinade on page 120.

CHANGING PROTEINS

If a recipe calls for chicken and you want to use beef, lamb, prawns, cod or paneer, do it! But this will change the cook times. Chicken cooks faster than beef or lamb. Paneer cooks faster than any meat, as do prawns or other types of seafood.

Substituting paneer: Paneer has a tendency to fall apart if cooked too long. Add it at the end of cooking and just let it heat through in the hot sauce. You could also fry the paneer in a little oil on all sides before mixing with the sauce, which will help it keep its shape and add more flavour.

Substituting red meat: Lamb, mutton and beef take longer to cook and become tender than poultry. If you are adapting a chicken recipe that calls for a three-hour cook on high, you will need to cook red meat for about an hour longer.

Substituting chicken: You can substitute chicken in any of these curries. I prefer to use chicken thigh meat as it has more flavour than breast meat and also holds its shape better. Breast meat can become a bit stringy if cooked too long, so watch it. Generally speaking, a chicken curry will take about an hour less to cook than a red meat curry.

Substituting seafood: Fish and seafood don't usually do well when cooked for a long time so you need to add them at the end of cooking. I suggest adding it to cook through in the last 30 minutes–1 hour of slow cooking.

Cooked meats: I have been asked whether you can use leftover grilled tandoori tikka instead of starting with raw meat. Although this idea might sound good to you, there are things to consider before adding cooked meats to your slow cooker. Don't ever add cooled, cooked meat, such as leftover tandoori chicken, to your slow cooker. The cooking process takes too long and harmful bacteria can grow, so cooked meats need to be heated up first in a microwave or pan until very hot, or until the internal temperature is 74°C (165°F) and added to the curry at the end.

Instead of cooked tandoori meat, you can marinate and then sear meat from raw. Use slightly larger pieces so that you can give it a good tandoori-style char while leaving the meat raw inside.

COOKING TIMES

Each recipe includes a preparation and cooking time but cooking times are notoriously variable – even more so in slow cooking – so remember to adjust as needed.

CHICKEN TIKKA MASALA

SERVES 4, OR MORE AS PART OF A MULTI-COURSE MEAL

This was the first curry I ever tested in my slow cooker. I had to test it a few times before I was happy with the recipe because I was adding way too much liquid and it tasted watery. The problem is now solved! If you like a good chicken tikka masala, you will love this one!

PREP TIME: 15 MINS
COOKING TIME: HIGH 3¼ HRS, LOW 6–8 HRS

2 tbsp ghee or rapeseed (canola) oil
800g (1lb 12oz) chicken breasts or thighs, cut into bite-sized pieces
2 onions, finely chopped
2 tbsp Garlic and ginger paste (page 120)
2 tbsp ground almonds
2 tbsp coconut milk powder
1 tbsp Curry powder or Mixed powder (page 118)
1½ tbsp sweet paprika
2 tbsp Tandoori masala (page 119)
½ tsp ground cumin
½ tsp ground coriander
1 tsp sugar, or to taste
200g (7oz) unseasoned passata
1 tbsp tomato paste
125ml (½ cup) shop-bought or homemade chicken stock (page 117) or water
Juice of 1 lemon
1 tbsp kasoori methi (dried fenugreek leaves)
Sea salt
1 tsp Garam masala (page 119)
1 tsp red food colouring powder (optional)
200ml (scant 1 cup) single (light) cream, or to taste
4 tbsp finely chopped coriander (cilantro) leaves, finely chopped

Heat the ghee or oil using the sauté/searing function of your slow cooker or in a pan over a medium–high heat. When the oil begins to glisten, add the chicken pieces in one layer and sear for a couple of minutes to brown. Transfer to a plate and set aside. Stir in the chopped onions and fry for about 5 minutes, or until soft and translucent.

Stir in the garlic and ginger paste and sauté for about 30 seconds to cook out the rawness.

Add the ground almonds, coconut milk powder, curry powder or mixed powder, paprika, tandoori masala, cumin, ground coriander and sugar. Your pot or pan will begin to look a bit dry, so pour in the passata, tomato paste and stock or water and bring to a simmer.

At this stage you can let the sauce cook as it is or blend everything using a stick or countertop blender until smooth, which will give you a creamy smooth sauce like you find at restaurants.

Stir the chicken into the sauce, secure the lid tightly and slow cook on the high setting for 3 hours or low for 6–8 hours until the chicken is cooked through.

Add the lemon juice and then add the kasoori methi by rubbing it between your fingers into the sauce, then season with salt to taste. Sprinkle over the garam masala and stir it in, then the red food colouring, if using.

Stir in the cream, a little at a time, until you are happy with the flavour and consistency. Be careful when doing this as you don't want the sauce to be too runny. Garnish with the coriander leaves to serve.

CHICKEN KORMA

SERVES 4, OR MORE AS PART OF A MULTI-COURSE MEAL

Mild, creamy and sweet... It's no wonder korma is a favourite with kids and anyone who shies away from spicy curries. As with all my recipes, be sure to taste this curry before serving and adjust the flavours to your own taste preferences. You can always add more sugar, for example, if you prefer your korma sweeter. As an exception to the usual rule, a korma is a delicate curry, so the chicken is usually added raw, without searing.

PREP TIME: 15 MINS
COOKING TIME: HIGH 3¼
HRS, LOW 6–8 HRS

3 tbsp rapeseed (canola) oil,
    coconut oil or ghee
5cm (2in) real cinnamon stick
2 green cardamom pods
2 onions, roughly chopped
1 tbsp Garlic and ginger paste
    (page 120)
1 tbsp sugar
2 tbsp ground almonds
2 tbsp tomato paste
250ml (1 cup) thick
    coconut milk
700g (1lb 9oz) chicken breasts
    and/or thighs, cut into
    bite-sized pieces
½ tsp rosewater (optional)
½ tsp Garam masala (page 119)
125ml (½ cup) double
    (heavy) cream
Sea salt
3 tbsp toasted flaked
    (slivered) almonds
    (optional), to garnish

Heat the oil or ghee using the sauté/searing function of your slow cooker or in a pan over a medium–high heat. When the oil begins to glisten, add the cinnamon stick and cardamom pods and let their flavours infuse into the oil for about 30 seconds.

Add the chopped onions and fry for about 5 minutes, or until soft and translucent.

Stir in the garlic and ginger paste and sauté for about 30 seconds, then stir in the sugar, ground almonds, tomato paste and coconut milk.

At this stage, remove and reserve the whole spices. Use a stick or countertop blender to blend the sauce until smooth. This step is optional but will give you a sauce that is much more like a curry-house-style korma sauce.

Transfer the sauce to your slow cooker, if necessary, then stir in the chicken pieces and return the whole spices to the sauce. Secure with the lid and cook on the high setting for 3 hours or low for 6–8 hours until the chicken is cooked through.

Stir in the rosewater, if using, and season with salt to taste. Stir in the garam masala. Swirl in the cream to taste and serve garnished with the toasted almond flakes, if using.

CHICKEN JALFREZI

SERVES 4, OR MORE AS PART OF A MULTI-COURSE MEAL

Traditionally, Jalfrezi curries are quick stir-fries. To make this work in a slow cooker you need to fry up the vegetables and put them aside to add to the curry at the end of cooking. You could just throw everything in your slow cooker and still get a decent curry but, as with most recipes in this book, the additional frying does come with flavour and texture benefits. Instead of adding the curry powder and other ground spices individually, you could use a few tablespoons of Jalfrezi paste (page 124).

PREP TIME: 15 MINS
COOKING TIME: HIGH 3¼ HRS, LOW 6–8 HRS

4 tbsp rapeseed (canola) oil or ghee
800g (1lb 12oz) chicken thighs or breasts, cut into bite-sized pieces
1 tsp black mustard seeds
½ tsp cumin seeds
20 fresh or frozen curry leaves
1 red onion, thinly sliced
2 green finger chillies, thinly sliced
½ green (bell) pepper, thinly sliced
½ red (bell) pepper, thinly sliced
½ yellow (bell) pepper, thinly sliced
3 tomatoes, quartered
1 onion, finely chopped
2 tbsp Garlic and ginger paste (page 120)
1 tbsp Curry powder or Mixed powder (page 118)
2 tsp Kashmiri chilli powder
1 tsp paprika
1 tsp ground cumin
1 tsp ground coriander
100ml (scant ½ cup) unseasoned passata
1 tbsp tomato paste
200ml (scant 1 cup) shop-bought or homemade chicken stock (page 117) or water
1 tsp kasoori methi (dried fenugreek leaves)
Sea salt, to taste
3 tbsp finely chopped coriander (cilantro)
2 limes, quartered

Heat 1 tablespoon of the oil in your slow cooker in the sauté/searing mode or in a pan over a medium–high heat. Add the chicken pieces in one layer and fry for a couple of minutes to brown. Transfer the chicken to a plate and set aside. Add 2 tablespoons of oil and, when hot, stir in the mustard seeds. When they start crackling, stir in the cumin seeds and curry leaves and let these sizzle in the oil for about a minute, stirring regularly.

Add the chopped red onion, finger chillies and peppers and fry for about 3 minutes so that the vegetables begin to char a little but are still fresh looking.

Add the tomatoes and fry for another minute. Pour or scoop it all into a bowl and set aside.

Add the remaining oil to the slow cooker or pan, stir in the chopped onion and fry, stirring regularly, for about 5 minutes, or until the onion is soft and translucent.

Stir in the garlic and ginger paste and fry for another minute. Stir in the curry or mixed powder, Kashmiri chilli powder, paprika, cumin, ground coriander, passata, tomato paste and chicken stock or water. At this stage, you can leave things as they are or blend these ingredients with a stick or countertop blender until smooth, which will give you a sauce that resembles the sauces you find at curry houses.

In your slow cooker, stir this sauce together with the chicken pieces, secure the lid and cook on the high setting for 3 hours or low for 6–8 hours until the chicken is cooked through.

Pour in the spices and vegetables you set aside earlier. Add the kasoori methi by rubbing the leaves between your fingers over the sauce, then season with salt to taste.

To finish, garnish with the chopped coriander and serve with the lime wedges to squeeze over the curry at the table.

CHICKEN DHANSAK

SERVES 4, OR MORE AS PART OF A MULTI-COURSE MEAL

Because of the nature of slow cooking and the fact that the ingredients cook in a moist environment while also releasing moisture themselves, I recommend that you pre-cook the lentils for this dhansak either on your stovetop or using my slow-cooker method (page 76). By adding the lentils cooked, it is easier to achieve the right thickness for the sauce. You can also blend them for a smoother sauce. If you are not a fan of pineapple in your dhansak, you can just leave it out, but I have included it in the recipe for those who like it.

PREP TIME: 15 MINS
COOKING TIME: HIGH 3¼
HRS, LOW 6–8 HRS

2 tbsp rapeseed (canola) oil
or ghee
700g (1lb 9oz) chicken
thighs or breasts, cut into
bite-sized pieces
2 onions, roughly chopped
2 tbsp Garlic and ginger paste
(page 120)
1 tsp ground turmeric
1 tbsp Curry powder or Mixed
powder (page 118)
1 tbsp Kashmiri chilli powder,
or to taste
1 tsp paprika
210ml (¾ cup) unseasoned
passata
50ml (3 tbsp) shop-bought or
homemade chicken stock
(page 117) or water
50ml (3 tbsp) pineapple juice
1 tbsp tamarind sauce or
concentrate
180g (1 cup) cooked red split
lentils (use packet
instructions)
3 tinned (canned) pineapple
rings, cut into small pieces
(optional)
1 tbsp lemon juice
Sea salt, to taste
3 tbsp finely chopped
coriander (cilantro)

Heat the oil in your slow cooker using the sauté/searing mode or in a pan over a medium–high heat. When the oil begins to shimmer, add the chicken pieces in one layer. You might need to sear the chicken in two batches. Brown the meat for about 4 minutes and then transfer to a plate and set aside. The chicken will not be cooked through at this stage. Stir in the chopped onions and fry, stirring regularly, for about 5 minutes, or until the onions are soft and translucent. You can add a drop more oil if needed.

Stir in the garlic and ginger paste and fry for another minute. Now add the turmeric, curry powder or mixed powder, Kashmiri chilli powder and paprika and stir into the onion mixture. Stir in the passata, chicken stock or water and the pineapple juice, then bring to a simmer. At this stage, you can leave things as they are or blend these ingredients with a stick or countertop blender until smooth. This is completely optional but will give you the smooth sauce you find at most curry houses.

Stir this sauce together with the chicken, tamarind sauce or concentrate and the cooked lentils, secure the lid and cook on the high setting for 3 hours or low for 6–8 hours until the chicken is cooked through.

Add the pineapple pieces, if using, and the lemon juice. Season with salt to taste. Serve garnished with the coriander.

CHICKEN REZALA

Rezala is similar to chicken tikka masala but it is spicier and calls for fewer ingredients. That said, you could use about 3 generous tablespoons of my Tikka masala paste (page 122) instead of adding the individual spices listed below. The flavour will be different but it will still be similar to a lot of the rezala curries you find on restaurant menus.

**PREP TIME: 15 MINS
COOKING TIME: HIGH 3¼ HRS, LOW 6–8 HRS**

2 tbsp rapeseed (canola) oil or ghee
3–4 green finger chillies, finely chopped
800g (1lb 12oz) chicken breast or thighs, cut into bite-sized pieces
3 onions, finely chopped
2 tbsp Garlic and ginger paste (page 120)
2 tbsp Mixed powder or Curry powder (page 118)
1 tsp Kashmiri chilli powder, or to taste
250ml (1 cup) unseasoned passata
70ml (¼ cup) shop-bought or homemade chicken stock (page 117) or water
½ tsp Garam masala (page 119)
125ml (½ cup) single (light) cream
Sea salt, to taste
3 tbsp finely chopped coriander (cilantro)
1–2 tbsp butter, diced
2 limes, quartered

Heat the oil in your slow cooker using the sauté/searing function or in a pan over a medium–high heat. When visibly hot, stir in the chopped chillies and fry for about a minute. Transfer the chillies to a plate using a slotted spoon and set aside.

Now add the chicken pieces in one layer in the pan. You might need to brown the chicken in batches. Don't overcrowd your pan or the chicken will stew rather than sear. Sear the meat for about 4 minutes all over and then transfer to a plate and set aside. The chicken will not be cooked through at this point. Stir the chopped onions into the pan and fry for about 5 minutes, or until soft and translucent. Transfer about half the onions to the plate with the chillies.

Stir the garlic and ginger paste into the remaining onions and fry for a further 30 seconds. Stir in the ground spices, passata and the chicken stock or water. At this point, you can blend these ingredients using a stick or countertop blender until smooth, which will give you a sauce that is closer to what you find at Indian restaurants, but this is completely optional.

Stir the chicken into the sauce in your slow cooker, secure the lid and cook on the high setting for 3 hours or low for 6–8 hours until the chicken is cooked through.

Stir in the reserved fried chillies and onion, along with the garam masala. Add the cream, a little at a time, until you are happy with the consistency of the sauce. Season with salt to taste and garnish with the chopped coriander and the butter, which will melt into the sauce. Serve with the lime wedges that can be squeezed over the top at the table.

BEEF MADRAS
SERVES 4

I love a good Madras curry, regardless of the protein used. Personally, I prefer using beef in a Madras, which I have done here. Feel free to use other proteins, though, as lamb and chicken are also very popular (see page 9 for cooking times). If you are considering making a Madras curry, you probably like a bit of a kick. This one isn't terribly spicy but you can always add more chilli powder, if you like, at the end of cooking. You can also use about 3–4 tablespoons of my homemade Madras paste (page 124) instead of adding the ground spices individually.

PREP TIME: 15 MINS
COOKING TIME: HIGH 4 HRS, LOW 6–8 HRS

3 tbsp rapeseed (canola) oil or ghee
700g (1lb 9oz) rump steak or stewing steak, cut into bite-sized pieces and seasoned with a little salt, to taste
2.5cm (1in) real cinnamon stick
2 dry Kashmiri chillies (optional)
2 cloves
Seeds from 2 green cardamom pods
2 onions, finely chopped
2–4 green finger chillies, finely chopped
2 tbsp Garlic and ginger paste (page 120)
½ tsp ground turmeric
2 tbsp ground cumin
2 tsp ground coriander
1 tbsp Mixed powder or Curry powder (page 118)
1–2 tbsp Kashmiri chilli powder
1 tsp paprika
200ml (scant 1 cup) passata
100ml (scant ½ cup) chicken stock (page 117), beef stock or water
1 tbsp tomato paste
1 tbsp smooth mango chutney, or to taste
½ tsp kasoori methi
½ tsp Garam masala (page 119)
Juice of ½ lime
Sea salt, to taste
3 tbsp finely chopped coriander (cilantro) leaves
2 limes, quartered

Heat 1 tablespoon of the oil in your slow cooker using the sauté/sear function or in a pan over a medium–high heat until the oil begins to shimmer and small bubbles begin to form. Add the beef pieces in one layer in the pan. You might need to brown the beef in batches. Don't overcrowd your pan or the beef will stew rather than sear. Sear the meat for about 4 minutes all over and then transfer to a plate and set aside. Pour in the remaining oil or ghee and, when shimmering from the heat, stir in the cinnamon stick, Kashmiri chillies, if using, the cloves and cardamom seeds and let them sizzle in the oil for about 30 seconds. Stir in the chopped onions and chillies and fry for about 5 minutes, or until the onions are soft and translucent.

Add the garlic and ginger paste and stir well for about 30 seconds to combine. Add the ground spices, passata, stock or water, tomato paste and mango chutney. At this point, you can leave this sauce as it is or blend it until smooth using a stick or countertop blender, which will give the sauce a smooth texture similar to what you find at Indian restaurants, but it is optional. If blending, remove the cinnamon stick first, then add it back for the slow-cooking process.

In your slow cooker, mix the sauce with the beef, secure the lid and cook on the high setting for 4 hours or low for 6–8 hours until the beef is mouthwateringly tender.

Add the kasoori methi by rubbing it between your fingers over the sauce and then stir in the garam masala. Squeeze in the lime juice and season with salt to taste before sprinkling with the coriander and serving with the lime wedges at the table to squeeze over the top.

*NOTE ABOUT REAL CINNAMON

This recipe calls for real or Ceylon cinnamon. Primarily grown in Sri Lanka, it is considered to be the best. The swirls of bark are paper thin and blend or even fall apart really well which gives the sauce a delicious flavour. The cheaper cassia has the same flavour, but thick bark that does not blend well. If using cassia bark, remove it before blending but return it to the pot for slow cooking.

BEEF KEEMA

SERVES 4

You will notice the flavour benefits of slow cooking keema in a grated onion and water mixture, searing the meat before you slow cook it. If you don't mind a few chunky bits of meat, you can skip the first step, but by spending the time to prepare it, you will get a much finer keema, like you find at the best restaurants. This recipe works with any ground meat so feel free to use chicken, turkey or lamb if you like.

PREP TIME: 15 MINS
COOKING TIME: HIGH 3¼
HRS, LOW 6–8 HRS

600g (1lb 5oz) minced (ground) beef
1 onion, grated
1 tsp sea salt
500ml (2 cups) water or beef stock
1 tbsp rapeseed (canola) oil or ghee

FOR THE CURRY

2 tbsp rapeseed (canola) oil or ghee
2 onions, finely chopped
2 tbsp Garlic and ginger paste (page 120)
1–2 green finger chillies, finely chopped, plus extra to serve
1–2 tbsp Mixed powder or Curry powder (page 118)
1 tsp ground cumin
1 tsp ground coriander
2 tsp Kashmiri chilli powder
1½ tsp ground turmeric
200ml (¾ cup) passata
100ml (scant ½ cup) water or meat stock
Sea salt, to taste
2 limes, quartered

Place the beef, onion and salt in a mixing bowl and pour over the water or stock. Mix well, breaking the meat apart as best you can with your hand. It should look like a meaty porridge. Set aside.

Using your slow cooker's sauté/searing function or in a large frying pan over a medium–high heat, heat the tablespoon of oil or ghee until it begins to shimmer and then pour in the meat mixture. Fry it for about 15 minutes or until almost all the water has dissolved, while stirring continuously to break down any chunks. Once the water has evaporated, continue to cook and brown the meat for a couple of minutes, then transfer the cooked keema and any cooking juices to a bowl and set aside.

Wipe your pan/pot clean – no need to make it spotless. Pour in the 2 tablespoons of oil for the curry, again on sauté /searing mode or in a pan over a medium–high heat. Add the chopped onions and fry for about 5 minutes, or until soft and translucent. Then stir in the garlic and ginger paste and the chopped chillies and continue frying for 30 seconds.

Stir in the ground spices and then pour in the passata and water or stock. Bring it all to a simmer, then add the cooked minced beef and meat juices.

In your slow cooker, cover it all tightly and cook on the high setting for 3 hours or on low for 6–8 hours. To finish, season with salt to taste. Serve with the quartered limes, which can be squeezed over the top at the table to taste, and a few extra green chillies sprinkled over.

CHICKEN CHILLI GARLIC
SERVES 4

Garlicky and spicy... what's not to like? This recipe is delicious exactly as written but if you want, you could use 3 to 4 tablespoons of homemade Madras paste (page 124). In fact, you could also use a combination of madras, vindaloo and tikka masala pastes, if you like. Any of these pastes work well in this curry.

PREP TIME: 10 MINS
COOKING TIME: HIGH 3
HRS, LOW 6–8 HRS

4 tbsp rapeseed (canola) oil
  or ghee
15 garlic cloves, cut into
  thin slivers
3 green finger chillies,
  thinly sliced
800g (1lb 12oz) chicken breast
  or thighs, cut into bite-sized
  pieces and lightly seasoned
  with salt, to taste
3 onions, finely chopped
½ tsp sea salt
2 tbsp Garlic and ginger paste
  (page 120)
1 tbsp Kashmiri chilli powder
1 tbsp Curry powder or Mixed
  powder (page 118)
2 tbsp Tandoori masala
  (page 119)
200ml (¾ cup) passata
100ml (scant ½ cup) shop-
  bought or homemade
  chicken stock (page 117)
  or water
1 tsp kasoori methi (dried
  fenugreek leaves)

TO GARNISH
Coriander (cilantro),
  chopped (optional)
More thinly sliced green
  chillies (optional)

Using your slow cooker in sauté/searing mode or a frying pan over a medium heat, heat the oil and add the garlic slivers. There's no need to wait until the oil is bubbling hot. Fry the garlic slivers until they are turning golden brown and are beginning to get a bit crispy. Just before the garlic is cooked to your liking, stir in the chopped chillies and fry for about 30 seconds. Using a slotted spoon, transfer the garlic and chillies onto a plate lined with paper towels, then set aside.

Add the chicken pieces in one layer in the pan. You might need to brown the chicken in batches. Don't overcrowd your pan or the chicken will stew rather than sear. Sear the meat for about 4 minutes all over and then transfer to a plate with a slotted spoon and set aside. The chicken will not be cooked through at this point.

Now add the chopped onions and salt to the oil and fry for about 7 minutes, or until the onion is translucent and beginning to turn golden brown. Transfer about one-third of the fried onions to the plate with the slivered garlic and chillies.

Stir the garlic and ginger paste into the remaining onions and fry, stirring continuously, for about a minute. To this, add the Kashmiri chilli powder, curry powder or mixed powder, and the tandoori masala and stir well to combine. Add the passata and the stock or water and bring to a simmer. At this point, you can either leave the sauce as it is or blend it until smooth using a stick or countertop blender. This will give you a sauce that is similar to the ones you find at curry houses, but blending is optional.

In your slow cooker, stir the chicken into the sauce, cover with the lid and cook on the high setting for 3 hours or low for 6–8 hours until the chicken is cooked through.

Hold back a little of the slivered garlic, chillies and onion to use as a garnish before pouring the rest into the cooker. Add the kasoori methi by rubbing the leaves between your fingers over the sauce, then season with salt to taste.

To serve, garnish with the reserved garlic, chillies and onion, the chopped coriander and more thinly sliced fresh green finger chillies, if you like.

LAMB ROGAN JOSH

SERVES 4, OR MORE AS PART OF A MULTI-COURSE MEAL

I would love you to try this rogan josh two ways. First give it a go exactly as written. Then make the Rogan josh paste (page 122) and use 3–4 tablespoons of that instead of the ground spices below. You will get similar but different results and I think you might even like the curry paste version best. The reason is that the spices are roasted whole and then ground, giving this and other curries more depth of flavour.

PREP TIME: 10 MINS
COOKING TIME: HIGH 4
HRS, LOW 6–8 HRS

8 cashews, soaked in hot water
    for 15 minutes
3 tbsp rapeseed (canola) oil
    or ghee
800g (1lb 12oz) lamb leg or
    shoulder, cut into bite-sized
    pieces and seasoned lightly
    with salt, to taste
2 onions, finely chopped
2 tbsp Garlic and ginger paste
    (page 120)
2½ tbsp smoked or
    unsmoked paprika
1 tsp Kashmiri chilli powder
1½ tbsp Mixed powder or Curry
    powder (page 118)
½ tsp ground cumin
½ tsp ground coriander
200g (7oz) tinned (canned)
    chopped tomatoes
100ml (scant ½ cup) shop-
    bought or homemade
    chicken stock (page 117),
    or meat stock or water
1 tsp kasoori methi (dried
    fenugreek leaves)
1 tsp Garam masala (page 119)
3 tbsp plain natural yogurt
2 tomatoes, quartered
Sea salt, to taste
3 tbsp finely chopped coriander
    (cilantro) leaves
Chopped red onion, to garnish

Drain the cashews, then pound them in a pestle and mortar with about 2 tablespoons of water to make a paste. You could also do this in a small food processor. Set aside.

Using your slow cooker in sauté/searing mode or a frying pan over a medium–high heat, heat the oil. When it begins to shimmer from the heat, add the lamb pieces in one layer in the pan. You might need to brown the lamb in batches. Don't overcrowd your pan or the lamb will stew rather than sear. Sear the meat for about 4 minutes all over and then transfer to a plate with a slotted spoon and set aside.

Stir in the chopped onions. Fry the onions for about 5 minutes, or until soft and translucent, then stir in the garlic and ginger paste and continue frying for another 30 seconds.

Now stir the ground spices into the onion mixture. Pour in the chopped tomatoes and stock or water and bring it all to a simmer. At this stage you can either leave the sauce as it is or blend it until smooth, which will give you a sauce that it more similar to curry-house-style sauces.

Stir the sauce and lamb together with the cashew paste you set aside earlier, until the lamb is completely coated, and then cook on the high setting for 4 hours or low for 6–8 hours, or until the meat is cooked through and tender.

When the meat is cooked to your liking, add the kasoori methi by rubbing it between your fingers over the sauce, then stir in the garam masala. Whisk in the yogurt, a tablespoon at a time, then add the tomato wedges. Push them right into the sauce to heat them through.

To finish, season with salt to taste and garnish with the coriander and red onion to serve.

LAMB NECK PASANDA

SERVES 4

Pasanda curries are great for kids and those who don't like too much heat. Like a curry-house-style korma, there are no spicy ingredients in this recipe. Traditionally, pasandas are prepared with flattened meat, which can either be sliced thinly or pounded. You could pound the meat with a meat mallet for appearance, if you like, but I usually don't bother. Lamb neck has a lot of muscle and loads of flavour but it needs to simmer for a good long time to become tender. You could use any cut of lamb but I wanted to show you that you can get amazing results with the cheapest cuts of lamb, so I used neck here.

PREP TIME: 10 MINS,
COOKING TIME: HIGH 4¼
HRS, LOW 6–8 HRS

3 tbsp rapeseed (canola) or
    coconut oil
4 tbsp flaked (slivered)
    almonds (optional
    to garnish)
800g (1lb 12oz) lamb neck or
    another cut of lamb, cut
    into bite-sized pieces and
    seasoned lightly with salt,
    to taste
2 onions, finely chopped
3 tbsp coconut milk powder
3 tbsp ground almonds
2 tbsp sugar
70ml (¼ cup) passata
70ml (¼ cup) meat stock
    or water
3 tbsp red wine or more
    stock or water
125ml (½ cup) thick
    coconut milk
1 heaped tbsp sultanas (golden
    raisins) or raisins
1 tsp Garam masala (page 119)
Sea salt, to taste
70ml (¼ cup) single (light)
    cream, or to taste

If toasting the almond flakes, heat the oil in your slow cooker using the sauté/searing function or in a pan over a medium–high heat. When the oil is looking bubbly hot, add the almond flakes and toast them, stirring continuously until lightly browned, which should only take a minute or so. Use a slotted spoon to transfer to a plate lined with paper towels and set aside.

Using the same oil, add the lamb pieces in one layer in the pan. You might need to brown the lamb in batches. Don't overcrowd your pan or the lamb will stew rather than sear. Sear the meat for about 4 minutes all over and then transfer to a plate with a slotted spoon and set aside.

Now stir in the chopped onions and fry for about 5 minutes or until soft and translucent. Stir in the coconut milk powder, ground almonds, sugar, passata, meat stock or water, wine and the thick coconut milk. Bring to a light simmer. At this point, you could leave the sauce as it is or blend it until smooth using a stick or countertop blender, just like the sauces you find at good curry houses.

In your slow cooker, stir the sultanas or raisins and lamb into the sauce. Cook on the high setting for 4 hours or 6–8 hours on low. When the meat is really tender, stir in the garam masala and add salt to taste. Slowly drizzle the cream over the curry to serve and then garnish with the toasted almond flakes, if using.

LAMB ACHARI
SERVES 4

Achari curries are some of my favourites because of the pickling spices used to make them. In this recipe, you use lime pickle and/or a combination of lime pickle and mango chutney, giving the sauce a depth of flavour that is to die for. The panch phoran pickling spice blend is available at Indian grocers and online and it is also easy to make. You simply mix equal measures of fennel seeds, fenugreek seeds, black mustard seeds, nigella seeds and cumin seeds. This recipe incorporates the pre-searing of the meat that gives that extra layer of flavour (page 6).

PREP TIME: 10 MINS
COOKING TIME: HIGH 4 HRS, LOW 6–8 HRS

4 tbsp rapeseed (canola) oil
1 tbsp panch phoran
2 dried Kashmiri chillies
1 red onion, thinly sliced
800g (1lb 12oz) lamb leg meat, cut into bite-sized pieces and seasoned lightly with salt, to taste
2 onions, finely chopped
2 tbsp Garlic and ginger paste (page 120)
2 green finger chillies, finely chopped
2 tbsp Mixed powder or Curry powder (page 118)
1 tsp ground coriander
2 tsp Kashmiri chilli powder
200ml (¾ cup) unseasoned passata
100ml (scant ½ cup) meat stock or water
2 tbsp lime pickle or 1 tbsp each of lime pickle and mango chutney
4 tbsp plain natural yogurt
1 tsp kasoori methi (dried fenugreek leaves)
1 tsp Garam masala (page 119)
Sea salt, to taste
Juice of 1 lime or lemon
3 tbsp finely chopped coriander (cilantro) leaves

Heat 2 tablespoons of the oil in your slow cooker using the sauté/searing mode or in a frying pan over a medium–high heat. When the oil begins to shimmer from the heat, stir in the panch phoran and dried Kashmiri chillies and stir these spices around in the oil for a minute or so, being careful not to burn them.

Add the sliced red onion and the lamb to the spices and stir well, searing the meat all over for a couple of minutes. Spoon the lamb, onions and spices into a bowl and set aside.

Add the remaining 2 tablespoons of oil to the slow cooker or pan and fry the chopped onions for about 7 minutes or until just beginning to turn a nice golden brown. Stir in the garlic and ginger paste and chopped chillies and fry them for another minute or so. Then stir in the mixed powder or curry powder, the ground coriander and the Kashmiri chilli powder along with the passata, the stock or water and either the 2 tablespoons of lime pickle or 1 tablespoon each of lime pickle and mango chutney. The mango chutney will give the curry a sweeter flavour.

At this stage you can leave the sauce as it is or blend it until smooth using a stick or countertop blender. Doing this will give you a smooth sauce similar to those you find at curry houses, but this step is optional.

Now stir the meat, onion, spices and chillies you set aside earlier into the sauce, then cover with the lid and cook on the high setting for 4 hours or low for 6–8 hours, or until the meat is really tender.

When the meat is cooked to your liking, begin whisking in the yogurt, a tablespoon at a time. Add the kasoori methi by rubbing the leaves between your fingers over the sauce, then stir in the garam masala.

Season with salt to taste and also squeeze in some lemon or lime juice to taste. Serve garnished with the chopped coriander.

CHICKEN CHASNI

SERVES 4

Chicken Chasni is the famous curry from Glasgow. It looks spicy hot because red food colouring is added to make it look so. It's actually quite mild. Many people don't like adding food colouring so it is optional. If you want it to look like a proper chasni though, it's got to go in.

PREP TIME: 10 MINS
COOKING TIME: HIGH 3¼
HRS, LOW 6–8 HRS

2 tbsp rapeseed (canola) oil
    or ghee
800g (1lb 12oz) chicken breast
    or thighs, cut into bite-sized
    pieces and seasoned lightly
    with salt, to taste
2 onions (about 250g/9oz),
    finely chopped
2 tbsp Garlic and ginger paste
    (page 120)
1 tsp ground cumin
1 tsp sweet paprika
¼ tsp ground turmeric
3 tbsp mango chutney
2 tbsp mint sauce
    (I use Colman's)
3 tbsp tomato ketchup
230ml (scant 1 cup)
    unseasoned passata
70ml (¼ cup) shop-bought or
    homemade chicken stock
    (page 117) or water
125ml (½ cup) single (light)
    cream, or to taste, plus extra
    to drizzle (optional)
Juice of 1 lemon, or to taste
¼ tsp Garam masala (page 119)
½ tsp red food colouring powder
    (optional but needed for a
    traditional chasni)
Sea salt, to taste
3 tbsp finely chopped coriander
    (cilantro), to garnish

Heat the oil or ghee in your slow cooker using the sauté/searing mode or in a frying pan over a medium heat. When the oil begins to glisten, add the chicken pieces in one layer in the pan. You might need to brown the chicken in batches. Don't overcrowd your pan or the chicken will stew rather than sear. Sear the meat for about 4 minutes all over and then transfer to a plate with a slotted spoon and set aside. The chicken will not be cooked through at this point.

Stir in the chopped onions and gently fry them for about 8 minutes. The idea here is to soften the onions and slowly bring out their natural sweetness without browning them. Add the garlic and ginger paste and fry for another minute or so, then stir in the cumin, paprika and turmeric. Add the mango chutney, mint sauce, ketchup, passata and stock or water and bring to a simmer. At this point you can leave the sauce as it is or blend it until smooth using a stick or countertop blender, which will give the sauce a more authentic, curry-house-style texture.

Mix this sauce and the chicken together in your slow cooker, cover with the lid and cook for 3 hours on the high setting or 6–8 hours on low.

When the chicken is cooked through, add the cream to your preference. You might only want to use half as much cream as called for and that's fine. Stir in the lemon juice to taste, the garam masala and food colouring, if using. Season with salt to taste and serve garnished with the chopped coriander and a drizzle of cream, if you like.

CHICKEN DOPIAZA
SERVES 4

Dopiaza curries offer rich and delicious flavours. Dopiaza means two onions or, in this case, onions cooked two ways. But every dopiaza recipe I've ever tried includes onions cooked in more ways than two and this recipe is no exception. You can purchase the crispy fried onions used as a garnish or fry some chopped onions in oil until crispy. It's an easy job but you might like the convenience of buying them.

PREP TIME: 15 MINS
COOKING TIME: HIGH 3¼ HRS, LOW 6–8 HRS

4 tbsp rapeseed (canola) oil or ghee
1 onion, quartered and broken up into individual petals
800g (1lb 12oz) chicken thighs, cut into bite-sized pieces and seasoned lightly with salt, to taste
2 onions, finely chopped
3 tbsp Garlic and ginger paste (page 120)
1 tbsp Curry powder or Mixed powder (page 118)
2 tsp ground cumin
1 tsp ground coriander
1 tsp paprika
1–2 tsp Kashmiri chilli powder
200g (7oz) chopped tinned (canned) tomatoes
100ml (scant ½ cup) shop-bought or homemade chicken stock (page 117) or water
1 tsp cumin seeds
1 tsp coriander seeds, roughly chopped
4 cardamom pods, bruised
2–4 green finger chillies, finely chopped
2 tbsp plain natural yogurt
6 tbsp finely chopped coriander (cilantro) leaves
½ tsp Garam masala (page 119)
Sea salt, to taste
5 tbsp crispy fried onions, homemade (page 51) or shop-bought, to garnish

Heat 1 tablespoon of the oil in your slow cooker using the sauté/searing function or in a pan on your stove over a medium–high heat. Place the onion petals in the pan and fry, turning regularly to char them in places. Transfer to a plate using a slotted spoon and set aside.

Add the chicken pieces in one layer in the pan. You might need to brown the chicken in batches. Don't overcrowd your pan or the chicken will stew rather than sear. Sear the meat for about 4 minutes all over and then transfer to a plate with a slotted spoon and set aside. The chicken will not be cooked through at this point.

Now add another 2 tablespoons of the oil to the pan and add the chopped onions. Fry for about 10 minutes, stirring often, until they are soft and deep golden brown in colour.

Stir in the garlic and ginger paste and fry for another 30 seconds. Then add the ground spices and stir again to coat the onions before pouring in the chopped tomatoes and stock or water and bringing to a simmer. At this point you can blend the sauce until smooth, like the sauces you get at curry houses, or leave it as it is for a chunkier texture. Pour it all into a bowl and set aside, and then clean your pan.

Pour in the remaining tablespoon of oil over a medium heat and, when the oil begins to shimmer from the heat, stir in the cumin seeds, coriander seeds, cardamom pods and green chillies to infuse for about 30 seconds. Stir in the sauce and bring to a simmer.

In your slow cooker, stir the chicken pieces and sauce together, cover with the lid and cook on the high setting for 3 hours or low for 6–8 hours until the chicken is cooked through.

Whisk in the yogurt, half the chopped coriander and the garam masala. Add the charred onion petals and stir them in well. Season with salt to taste and serve garnished with the remaining chopped coriander and the crispy fried onions.

LAMB VINDALOO
SERVES 4

If you like a good, spicy curry, you can't go wrong with this vindaloo. That said, the spicing is down to you. Although this isn't the spiciest vindaloo I've made, it does have a good kick to it. Feel free to use less chilli powder and fewer chillies, if you like. Or you can increase the amounts if you want to make this lava hot! You can also make the Vindaloo paste (page 123) and add 3 to 4 tablespoons of it instead of adding the ground spices individually.

PREP TIME: 10 MINS
COOKING TIME: HIGH 4¼
HRS, LOW 6–8 HRS

4 tbsp rapeseed (canola) oil
800g (1lb 12oz) lamb leg or
    shoulder, cut into bite-sized
    pieces
2 onions, finely chopped
2 tbsp Garlic and ginger paste
    (page 120)
1 tsp ground turmeric
2 tbsp Kashmiri chilli powder
1 tbsp ground cumin
1 tbsp ground coriander
1 tsp paprika
1 tsp Garam masala (page 119)
1 tsp ground black pepper
1 tbsp Mixed powder or Curry
    powder (page 118)
1 tsp sugar, or to taste
200g (7oz) tinned (canned)
    chopped tomatoes
100ml (scant ½ cup) meat stock
    or water
3 green cardamom pods,
    lightly bruised
2 star anise
1 Indian bay leaf (cassia leaf)
2 green finger chillies,
    finely chopped
2 scotch bonnet chillies,
    finely chopped
1 potato, peeled and cut into
    bite-sized pieces
2 tbsp white distilled vinegar
1 tsp kasoori methi (dried
    fenugreek leaves)
Sea salt, to taste
3 tbsp finely chopped
    coriander (cilantro)
2 limes, quartered, to serve

Using your slow cooker in sauté/searing mode or a frying pan over a medium–high heat, heat 2 tablespoons of the oil or ghee. When it begins to shimmer from the heat, add the lamb pieces in one layer in the pan. You might need to brown the lamb in batches. Don't overcrowd your pan or the lamb will stew rather than sear. Sear the meat for about 4 minutes all over and then transfer to a plate with a slotted spoon and set aside.

Returning to your pan, stir in the chopped onions and fry for about 7 minutes, or until soft and light golden brown in colour. Stir in the garlic and ginger paste and fry for about 30 seconds, then add the ground spices, moving the spices around in the pan until the onions are nicely coated. Add the sugar, chopped tomatoes and stock or water and bring it to a simmer. At this point you can leave the sauce as it is or blend it until smooth so that it is closer to the sauces you find in restaurants.

Either way, for best results, pour the sauce into a bowl and wipe your pot or pan clean. Pour in the remaining 2 tablespoons of oil and, when it is glistening and hot, stir in the cardamom pods, star anise, Indian bay leaf and chillies and stir them around in the oil for about a minute. Then add the sauce, lamb and potatoes and stir well to combine.

Cover with the lid and cook on the high setting for 4 hours or low for 6–8 hours, or until the lamb and potatoes are good and tender.

To finish, stir in the vinegar and add the kasoori methi by rubbing it between your fingers. Check for seasoning and add salt to taste. You can also add more sugar, chillies and/or chilli powder at this stage, again to taste. Just let these simmer in the sauce for about 5 minutes. Serve hot, topped with chopped coriander and the quartered limes for additional sour flavour.

BUTTER CHICKEN

SERVES 4

Butter chicken is usually made with grilled tandoori chicken, and the creamy yogurt marinade is mixed with cream to make the sauce. This version is quite a lot easier but you still get a very good, if perhaps less authentic, butter chicken.

**PREP TIME: 15 MINS
COOKING TIME: HIGH 3
HRS, LOW 6–8 HRS**

1kg (2lb 4oz) chicken thighs, skinned and cut into small pieces

FOR THE MARINADE

Juice of 1 large lemon
2 tbsp rapeseed (canola) oil
1 level tsp sea salt
1 tbsp Garlic and ginger paste (page 120)
1 tbsp Kashmiri chilli powder
1 tsp ground cumin
1 tsp ground coriander
½ tsp ground turmeric
1 generous tsp Tandoori masala (page 119)

FOR THE SAUCE

15 raw cashews, soaked in water for 15 minutes
250ml (1 cup) passata
2 tbsp ghee or rapeseed (canola) oil
2 medium red onions, blended with 2 tbsp water if needed
2 tbsp Garlic and ginger paste (page 120)
1 tsp Kashmiri chilli powder or paprika
1 tsp ground cumin
1 tsp ground coriander
½ tsp sugar, or to taste
100g (4oz) butter
200ml (¾ cup) double (heavy) cream, whisked
1 tbsp kasoori methi (dried fenugreek leaves)
½ tsp Garam masala (page 119)
Sea salt, to taste

Whisk all the marinade ingredients together in a large mixing bowl. Add the chicken pieces and stir them in to coat. Allow to marinate for 30 minutes or up to 4 hours but no longer! Strain the soaked raw cashews and blend them with the passata for the sauce together until smooth. Set aside.

When ready to cook, heat the ghee or oil in your slow cooker using the sauté/searing mode or in a pan over a medium–high heat. When it begins to bubble lightly, remove as much of the marinade from the chicken as you can and retain all the marinade. Sauté the chicken in one layer for about 5 to 7 minutes to lightly char the exterior. Transfer to a plate using a slotted spoon. The chicken will not be cooked through at this point.

Now stir in the blended onions and fry for about 5 minutes to cook out the raw flavour. Then stir in the garlic and ginger paste and fry for an additional minute. Stir in the chilli powder or paprika, cumin, ground coriander and sugar, then pour in the blended passata and cashews and bring to a simmer. Stir in the chicken and all the marinade. Bring back to a simmer.

In your slow cooker, put on the lid and cook for 3 hours on the high setting or 6–8 hours on low until the chicken is cooked through.

Stir in the butter and let it melt into the sauce. Then add the whisked cream (you don't have to add it all if you don't want to). Add the kasoori methi by rubbing it between your fingers over the sauce, then stir in the garam masala. Season with salt to taste just before serving.

PRAWN PATHIA

SERVES 4

Although chicken pathia is more popular than prawn pathia, I wanted to show you a good way to add prawns and other seafood to a slow-cooker curry with this recipe. You could definitely add chicken instead and the curry will take about the same amount of time to cook. When adding prawns and other seafood, you only want to add them about an hour before the cook is finished or they will overcook. For extra flavour, I recommend making my Fish stock (page 117) but you could just go with water or chicken stock, or even a seafood stock made with a stock cube. You can use unpeeled prawns for more flavour but it will be messier to eat.

**PREP TIME: 10 MINS
COOKING TIME: HIGH 2
HRS, LOW 4 HRS**

2 tbsp rapeseed (canola) oil
2 onions, finely chopped
2 tbsp Garlic and ginger paste
    (page 120)
2 tbsp Curry powder or Mixed
    powder (page 118)
1 tsp Kashmiri chilli powder
230ml (scant 1 cup)
    unseasoned passata
70ml (¼ cup) shop-bought
    or homemade fish stock or
    chicken stock (page 117),
    or water
2 tbsp sugar
½ tsp tamarind concentrate
1 tbsp mango chutney
800g (1lb 12oz) peeled raw
    prawns (shrimp) (or see
    intro)
1 tsp kasoori methi (dried
    fenugreek leaves)
Juice of 1–2 lemons
Sea salt, to taste
3 tbsp chopped coriander
    (cilantro) leaves

Heat the oil in your slow cooker using the sauté/searing function or in a pan over a medium–high heat. When the oil begins to shimmer, stir in the chopped onions and fry for 5 minutes, or until soft and translucent. Add the garlic and ginger paste, stir it into the onions and fry for a further minute.

Stir in the curry powder or mixed powder and Kashmiri chilli powder and then add the passata, stock or water, sugar, tamarind concentrate and mango chutney and bring it all to a simmer. At this point you can leave the sauce as it is or blend it using a stick or countertop blender to achieve a smoother sauce like you find at curry houses.

Add the sauce to your slow cooker, then cover with the lid and cook the sauce on the high setting for 2 hours or low for about 4 hours. Stir in the prawns and let them cook into the sauce for the last hour of cooking. Watch them, though, as slow cookers do vary, as do the size of prawns, and you don't want to overcook them. They are ready when white all the way through and not at all transparent or raw looking.

When the prawns are cooked through, add the kasoori methi by rubbing it between your fingers over the sauce. Add lemon juice and salt to taste and garnish with the chopped coriander to serve.

NOTE

If you decide to make this with chicken or lamb, you will make it just as the previous recipes, searing the chicken or lamb and then preparing the sauce. Then you will cook it for the suggested times in those recipes.

TRADITIONAL INDIAN RECIPES

Here you will find some of the most famous and popular authentic Indian-style curries and other main dishes. Slow cooking is perfect for these recipes as most are traditionally stewed for a few hours anyway in a pot on the stove. You're just doing it in a slow cooker instead of a pot.

LAMB NIHARI
SERVES 4–6

You can choose the cuts of lamb you want to use for this recipe. Use only lamb shanks or perhaps go with shanks and some shoulder. This is also good made with stewing beef, as it is seared before slow cooking. You will need about 1kg (2lb) meat not including the bones, regardless of what you choose. This is a delicious curry that is served at the table with chopped coriander (cilantro), lemon wedges, julienned ginger and chopped green chillies to taste.

PREP TIME: 5 MINS
COOKING TIME: HIGH 4
HRS, LOW 6–8 HRS

70ml (¼ cup) rapeseed (canola)
    oil or ghee
2 onions, thinly sliced
2 tbsp Garlic and ginger paste
    (page 120)
2 lamb shanks and 500g
    (1lb 2oz) lamb shoulder,
    cut into bite-sized pieces
½ tsp sea salt, plus extra
    to taste

FOR THE SPICE BLEND
1 whole nutmeg, crushed
    into small pieces
1 blade of mace
2 tbsp fennel seeds
3 Indian bay leaves (cassia
    leaves), shredded
2.5cm (1in) real cinnamon stick
    or cassia bark, broken into
    small pieces
1 tsp black peppercorns
1 tsp nigella seeds (black
    onion seeds)
1 tsp cloves
2 tsp cumin seeds
1 tsp paprika
1 tsp hot chilli powder
1 tsp ground ginger
2 generous tbsp chapati flour*

TO SERVE
Rice, chapatis or rumali roti
5cm (2in) piece of root ginger,
    peeled and julienned
2–3 hot fresh green chillies,
    finely sliced
I handful of coriander
    (cilantro) leaves
Lemon wedges

Place all the whole spices for the blend in a spice grinder and grind to a fine powder. There is no need to roast them first when making a nihari. Add the paprika, chilli powder, ginger and chapati flour and blend again to combine. Set aside.

Heat the oil or ghee in your slow cooker using the sauté/searing mode or in a pan over a medium–high heat and add the sliced onions. Fry for about 8 minutes or until soft, brown and translucent.

Stir in the garlic and ginger paste and fry for another minute. Season the meat with the salt and add it to the pot. Stir regularly for about 5 minutes to brown the meat and then add the nihari spice blend. Stir well so the meat is completely coated with the spice blend and then add 500ml (2 cups) of water.

Cover with the lid and set your slow cooker to the high setting for 4 hours or low for 6–8 hours. Push the meat down as much as you can into the liquid. The meat will reduce in size as it cooks and there will be more gravy when finished, so don't be tempted to add more liquid.

When the meat is fall-apart tender, lift the lid. If it is too watery, you can reduce it down using the sauté/searing function of your slow cooker with the lid off, or in a pan. The sauce should be quite thick thanks to the flour in the spice blend. Season with salt to taste and serve over rice or with chapatis or rumali roti. Serve with the ginger, green chillies, coriander leaves and lemon wedges, which can be added to taste at the table.

*NOTE
This is the only recipe in the book that isn't gluten free because of the chapati flour in the sauce. If you are gluten free, you can substitute 3–4 tablespoons of cornflour (cornstarch).

LAMB MAPPAS

This is a really different and delicious curry that I tried many times around Kerala. It's often served as part of an elaborate breakfast, but if curry for breakfast isn't your thing, it's very nice for dinner too. There is a heavy use of ground coriander in this curry, which is what makes it unique. I always say to use the freshest ingredients you can, but that is especially true for this curry, where the ground coriander absolutely needs to be at its best! You might even want to roast whole coriander seeds until warm to the touch and fragrant, then grind them to a powder yourself. That ground coriander is the star of the sauce.

PREP TIME: 10 MINS
COOKING TIME: HIGH 4 HRS, LOW 6–8 HRS

3 tbsp coconut or rapeseed (canola) oil
30 fresh or frozen curry leaves
2 red onions, finely chopped
2 green chillies, finely chopped
5cm (2in) piece of root ginger, finely chopped
10 garlic cloves, finely chopped
200ml (7oz) tinned (canned) chopped tomatoes
1–2 tbsp Kashmiri chilli powder
4 tbsp ground coriander
1 tsp ground turmeric
1 tsp black pepper
1.5kg (3lb 5oz) lamb or mutton leg or shoulder on the bone, cut into small pieces (and seared in the hot oil (page 6) if you wish)
250ml (1 cup) coconut milk
Sea salt, to taste

Heat the oil in your slow cooker using the sauté/searing function or in a large pan on your stove over a medium–high heat. When hot, add the curry leaves and infuse them in the oil for about 30 seconds. Add the chopped red onions and fry over a medium heat for about 7 minutes, or until turning light brown in colour.

Now stir in the green chillies, ginger and garlic and give it another good stir. Then add the chopped tomatoes and ground spices and stir well to combine. Add the meat and coconut milk and stir well to coat the meat completely. Slow cook on high for 4 hours or on low for 6–8 hours with the lid on. Season with salt to taste and serve immediately.

RAILWAY LAMB
SERVES 4

Railway lamb curry was first made popular in the first-class dining cars in India during the British Raj. The lamb or mutton curry that was served originally was a bit spicy for the British palate at the time, so fewer chillies were used and coconut milk or yogurt was added to calm the heat, but you can make this as spicy as you like.

PREP TIME: 15 MINS
COOKING TIME: HIGH 4¼
HRS, LOW 6–8 HRS

5 tbsp (¼ cup) mustard oil
5 cardamom pods, bruised
3 Kashmiri dried red chillies
4 cloves
2.5cm (1in) real cinnamon stick
20 fresh or frozen curry leaves
2 red onions, finely chopped
3 green chillies, finely chopped
2 tbsp Garlic and ginger paste
    (page 120)
1 tsp Kashmiri chilli powder
½ tsp ground turmeric
1 tbsp ground coriander
1 tbsp cumin
200g (7oz) chopped tomatoes
1 tbsp tomato paste
1kg (2lb 3oz) mutton or lamb
    shoulder on the bone,
    cut into bite-sized pieces
    (and seared in the hot oil
    (page 6) if you wish)
3 potatoes, peeled and
    quartered
200ml (scant 1 cup) thick
    coconut milk
1 generous tsp tamarind
    concentrate
1 tsp kasoori methi (dried
    fenugreek leaves)
Sea salt, to taste
Chopped coriander (cilantro),
    to garnish (optional)
2 limes, quartered, to serve

Heat the oil in your slow cooker using the sauté/searing mode or in a pan over a medium–high heat. When the oil begins to bubble, stir in the cardamom pods, dried chillies, cloves, cinnamon stick and the curry leaves and let them sizzle in the oil for about 30 seconds. Stir in the red onions and fry for about 5 minutes until the onions are soft and translucent. Then add the chopped chillies and the garlic and ginger paste and fry, stirring continuously, for a further 30 seconds.

Now add the ground spices and stir them into the onions for about a minute, followed by the chopped tomatoes and tomato paste. Add the meat, potatoes, coconut milk and tamarind concentrate and stir it all well to combine. Bring to a low simmer.

Cook it all in your slow cooker, covered with the lid, for 4 hours on the high setting or 6–8 hours on low. You want the meat and potatoes to be good and tender before serving so check them with a fork and cook a little longer if necessary.

Once cooked, add the kasoori methi by rubbing it between your fingers over the curry. Stir it in and add salt to taste. Garnish with the chopped coriander. I usually serve this with rice and a few lime wedges that can be squeezed over the curry to taste at the table, but as there are potatoes in the curry, you could just serve it on its own without rice.

LAMB DUM BIRYANI

SERVES 6–8

This amazing biryani can be a bit labour intensive but there are a couple of cheats to make things easier. You could use 450g (1lb) of shop-bought crispy fried onions – or make them in advance – rather than frying them yourself. You could also purchase about 1kg (2lb 4oz) of cooked white basmati rice, but you will get better results if you use good-quality uncooked basmati rice and cook it as below. So if you want ease of cooking, cheat! If you want perfection, cook!

PREP TIME: 25 MINS,
PLUS MARINATING
COOKING TIME: HIGH 4½
HRS, LOW 6–8 HRS

1 leg of lamb, cut through the
    bone into 12 or more pieces

FOR THE MARINADE
2 tbsp Garlic and ginger paste
    (page 120)
420g (1¾ cups) plain yogurt
Juice of 2 lemons
2 fresh green chillies, chopped
1 tbsp ground cumin
1 tbsp Garam masala (page 119)
½ tsp ground turmeric
1 tsp ground cinnamon
¼ tsp ground mace
½ tsp chilli powder
30g (1oz) coriander (cilantro)
    leaves, finely chopped
10g (⅓oz) mint leaves,
    finely chopped

FOR THE BIRYANI
250ml (1 cup) rapeseed
    (canola) oil
3 onions, thinly sliced
500g (1lb 2oz) basmati rice
6 tbsp melted ghee
Pinch of saffron
2 tsp sea salt
Whole-spice garam masala:
    5cm (2in) real cinnamon
    stick, 10 peppercorns, 1 bay
    leaf, 1 tbsp cumin seeds
60g (2oz) coriander (cilantro)
    leaves, finely chopped
20g (¾oz) mint leaves,
    finely chopped
2 tsp rosewater (optional)

Start by cooking the crispy onions. This can be done in advance and kept in an airtight container in the fridge for 1–2 days. Heat the oil in your slow cooker using the sauté/sear function or in a large pan over a medium–high heat. The oil is hot enough when a couple of slices of onion sizzle and rise to the top on contact. Add the sliced onions and fry for 15 minutes, or until crispy and deep golden brown. You might need to do this in batches. Transfer the crispy fried onions to a plate lined with paper towels, reserving the cooking oil. Set aside.

Pour the rice into a bowl and cover with water. Swirl the rice around with your hand. The water will become milky. Pour the water out and repeat about 5 times, or until the water is almost clear. Strain, then cover with fresh water to soak while you are cooking the biryani. Whisk in the melted ghee and saffron and leave to soak and infuse.

In a bowl, whisk all the marinade ingredients together until smooth, then add a quarter of the fried onions and 5 tablespoons of the oil used to cook them. Add the lamb to the marinade and leave in your fridge for up to 72 hours. The longer the better.

Cook the marinated meat and all the marinade in your slow cooker, with the lid on, for 4 hours on high or 6–8 hours on low.

About an hour before the meat sauce is ready, boil 1.5 litres (6⅔ cups) of water in a large pan. Add the salt and whole garam masala. Strain the rice, add to the pan and simmer for 6 minutes.

Remove half the rice from the water, strain, then place in a small bowl. Cook the remaining rice for another minute, then strain it into a second bowl. Set aside. Leave the whole spices in the rice.

About an hour before the finished cooking time, season the meat with salt to taste and cover it with the rice you took out of the water after 6 minutes. Top this with half the herbs, 1 teaspoon of rosewater, if using, and half the remaining fried onions. Drizzle half of the saffron-infused ghee over the top. Top this with the remaining rice and add the remaining herbs, onions, rosewater and saffron ghee. Cover and continue cooking for another hour or so.

To serve, lightly stir the biryani, bringing some of the meat to the top. Do not stir too vigorously or the rice grains will split. Delicious served with whisked plain yogurt or a good raita.

SRI LANKAN BLACK CHICKEN CURRY

SERVES 4

You can purchase Sri Lankan black curry powder if you wish, but with this recipe I show you how to make your own using chilli powder and normal curry powder. If you do make it, you can do this a couple of days ahead of cooking. The optional marinating of the chicken and frying the whole spices, onion and other aromatics can also be done a couple of days ahead of slow cooking. Then just throw it all in your slow cooker and let it gently simmer until the chicken is cooked through.

PREP TIME: 15 MINS
COOKING TIME: HIGH 3¼
HRS, LOW 6–8 HRS

2 tbsp Kashmiri chilli powder
2 tbsp good-quality
   curry powder
1 kg (1¼lb) small chicken
   thighs, skin removed and
   preferably on the bone
1 tsp sea salt
1 tsp black pepper
1 tbsp light soy sauce*
   or tamari (GF)
4 tbsp coconut oil
1 real cinnamon stick, broken
   into small pieces, or cassia
   bark, left whole
4 cloves
2 cardamom pods,
   lightly bruised
2 green chillies, cut lengthways
5 garlic cloves, finely chopped
2.5cm (1in) piece of root ginger,
   finely chopped
2 small pieces of pandan leaf
   about 7.5cm (3in) square total
20 fresh or frozen curry leaves
½ medium red onion,
   finely chopped
½ tsp ground turmeric
1 tsp Chinese chicken powder
   (optional but it adds a
   nice flavour)
300ml (1¼ cups) shop-bought
   or homemade chicken stock
   (page 117) or water

If making the Sri Lankan black curry powder, place a dry frying pan over a medium heat or set your slow cooker on sauté/sear mode and stir in the Kashmiri chilli powder. Toast the chilli powder for a few minutes, stirring often, until it turns a deep chocolate colour. Transfer the toasted chilli powder to a bowl and then repeat with the curry powder. Mix the two powders together.

Put the chicken in a large mixing bowl and season with the salt, pepper and soy sauce or tamari. Be sure to mix these ingredients right into the flesh of the meat. You can now go straight to cooking or leave it to marinate overnight. The longer the better.

When ready to cook, heat the coconut oil in your slow cooker using the sauté/searing mode or a pan over a medium–high heat. Add the cinnamon stick, cloves, cardamom pods, chillies, garlic, ginger, pandan leaf and curry leaves and stir it all up. Let them infuse into the oil for about a minute.

Stir in the chopped onion and continue frying for about 7 minutes, or until the onion is just beginning to turn a golden brown. Stir in the ground turmeric, the chicken stock powder, if using, and the roasted curry powder and chilli powder blend.

Pour in the chicken stock or water and bring it all to a simmer. Then add the chicken and stir it all to combine. Cook, covered with the lid, in your slow cooker on the high setting for 3 hours or low for 6–8 hours. Check the chicken for doneness, season with salt and pepper to taste and enjoy with white rice.

*NOTE
Many soy sauces contain gluten but there are gluten-free brands available.

SOUTH INDIAN-STYLE CHICKEN CURRY

SERVES 4

South Indian curries are some of my favourites. I love the fresh flavours and the coconut milk sauce that is popular in so many of them. As slow cooker curries go, this one is really simple and perhaps a good one to begin your slow cooker curry journey with.

PREP TIME: 15 MINS
COOKING TIME: HIGH 3
HRS, LOW 6–8 HRS

2 tbsp rapeseed (canola)
    or coconut oil
5cm (2in) real cinnamon stick
10 black peppercorns
6 green cardamom pods,
    lightly crushed
20 fresh or frozen curry leaves
2 medium red onions, very
    finely chopped
10 green finger chillies, finely
    chopped (to taste, optional)
1kg (2lb 2oz) skinless
    chicken thighs, cut
    into bite-sized pieces
½ tsp ground turmeric
2 tsp ground coriander
1 tsp ground cumin
2 tomatoes, finely diced
200ml (¾ cup) thick
    coconut milk
½ tsp Garam masala (page 119)
Sea salt and freshly ground
    black pepper
Lime juice, to garnish
4 tbsp chopped coriander
    (cilantro), to garnish

FOR THE CHILLI PASTE
70ml (¼ cup) shop-bought or
    homemade fish or chicken
    stock (page 117) or water
12 green bird's eye chillies
2 garlic cloves, peeled
1 medium red onion,
    roughly chopped
1 large bunch (60g/2oz) of
    coriander (cilantro), chopped
Juice of 1 lime

Place all the chilli paste ingredients in a blender and blend to a thick paste. Try not to add more liquid than called for unless absolutely needed to assist blending. Set aside.

Heat the oil in your slow cooker using the sauté/searing mode or in a pan over a medium–high heat on your stove. Stir in the whole spices, curry leaves and chopped onions and fry for about 8 minutes, or until soft, translucent and turning a golden brown. Stir in the chopped chillies, if using, and fry for another minute.

Now add the chicken pieces, the turmeric, ground coriander, cumin and the chilli paste and stir well to combine. Add the diced tomatoes and the coconut milk and stir well to combine. Bring to a simmer.

Cook in your slow cooker, covered with the lid, on the high setting for 3 hours or low for 6–8 hours.

When your curry is cooked, stir in the garam masala, then season with salt and pepper to taste. A good squeeze of lime juice is also nice. Garnish with the chopped coriander, then serve over basmati rice and enjoy.

JEERA CHICKEN

SERVES 4

The star ingredient in this recipe is the cumin so, for best results, it is important to roast and grind the cumin seeds yourself rather than just using ground cumin off the shelf. You will get a much deeper flavour, which this curry is famous for.

PREP TIME: 15 MINS
COOKING TIME: HIGH 3½
HRS, LOW 6–8 HRS

4 tbsp cumin seeds
70ml (¼ cup) rapeseed
  (canola) oil
1 onion, thinly sliced
1 generous tbsp Garlic and
  ginger paste (page 120)
2 green bird's eye chillies,
  finely chopped, plus extra to
  serve (optional)
½ tsp ground turmeric
½ tsp Kashmiri chilli powder
1 tsp ground coriander
1 tbsp Garam masala (page 119)
250ml (1 cup) shop-bought or
  homemade chicken stock
  (page 117) or water, plus
  1–2 tbsp
800g (1lb 12oz) chicken,
  cut into bite-sized pieces
2–3 generous tbsp natural
  plain yogurt
Sea salt, to taste
3 tbsp finely chopped
  coriander leaves (optional),
  to garnish

Toast 2 tablespoons of the cumin seeds in a dry frying pan over a medium heat or in a slow cooker using the searing/sauté mode until fragrant and warm to the touch but not yet smoking. Be careful not to burn the cumin or it will become bitter. Grind the cumin in a mortar or spice grinder into a fine powder and set aside.

Heat the oil in your slow cooker using the sauté/searing function or in a pan over a medium–high heat on your stove. When the oil begins to shimmer, add the onion and fry for about 10 minutes until golden brown in colour but not burnt. Use a slotted spoon to transfer the fried onions to a plate lined with paper towels to soak up any excess oil. You only need 2 tablespoons of oil for the curry so you can discard some of it or leave it in for a more traditional flavour and texture.

Reduce the heat to medium and add the remaining 2 tablespoons of cumin seeds to the oil and fry for about 20 seconds to infuse their flavour into the oil. Stir in the garlic and ginger paste and fry for about 30 seconds, just to cook off the rawness. Add the chopped chillies and the turmeric, chilli powder, ground coriander, garam masala and ground cumin and stir well to combine.

Your pan will look quite dry from the spices so add 1–2 tablespoons of water (or stock) so that they don't burn. Stir in the chicken and fry for about 3 minutes to brown lightly in the oil and spice mixture. Return all but a couple of tablespoons of the fried onions to the pan, add the stock or water and stir well to combine.

In your slow cooker, cook the curry, with the lid on, on the high setting for 3 hours or low for 6–8 hours until the chicken is cooked through.

Whisk in the yogurt, one tablespoon at a time. Season with salt to taste and garnish with fresh coriander, the remaining fried onions and the fresh green chillies, if using, to serve.

SALMON MOLEE

SERVES 4

Molee curries are some of the best seafood curries out there. I have used salmon for this recipe but you could use any meaty fish. Although I usually add seafood and fish at the end of cooking, you should find that the large salmon fillets cook perfectly well in the sauce for the whole cook. If you find that the salmon is cooked through before the suggested cooking time, serve the curry or stop slow cooking and hit the keep warm button if you have one.

PREP TIME: 15 MINS
COOKING TIME: LOW
2–3 HRS

2 tbsp coconut oil
1 tbsp black mustard seeds
20 fresh or frozen curry leaves
1 onion, finely chopped
2 tbsp Garlic and ginger paste
(page 120)
2–5 fresh green chillies,
finely chopped (to taste)
1½ tsp Kashmiri chilli powder
½ tsp ground cumin
1 tsp ground turmeric
2 tomatoes, finely chopped
400ml (1¾ cups) thick
coconut milk
4 x 200g (7oz) salmon fillets
Sea salt and freshly ground
black pepper, to taste
4 tbsp finely chopped
coriander (cilantro),
to garnish (optional)
2 limes, quartered
White rice, to serve

Heat the oil in your slow cooker using the sauté/searing function or in a pan over a medium–high heat. Stir in the mustard seeds and when they begin to crackle, stir in the curry leaves and chopped onion and fry for about 5 minutes, or until the onion is soft and translucent.

Add the garlic and ginger paste and chopped chillies and fry for another minute, stirring regularly. Stir in the chilli powder, cumin and turmeric. Then add the chopped tomatoes and fry for another minute. Pour in the coconut milk and bring it all to a simmer.

In your slow cooker, add the salmon fillets to the sauce. Try to arrange the salmon so that it is in one layer. Cover and cook on low for 2–3 hours, or until the salmon is cooked through. Some slow cookers only allow you to slow cook on low for a minimum of 4 hours. If this is the case with your model, set it for 4 hours and then turn it off when the fish is cooked.

To finish, season with salt and pepper to taste and garnish with the chopped coriander, if using. Serve with lime wedges at the table, which can be squeezed over the curry to taste. This curry is great served simply over white rice.

TANDOORI CHICKEN

SERVES 3–4

Some might wonder why you would ever want to cook tandoori chicken in a slow cooker. When I decided to give it a try, my wife and I were going out for a few hours. We marinated the chicken and placed it on the high setting in our slow cooker to cook. When we returned home, the meat was cooked through and succulent. The meat can be used in wraps, sandwiches and salads. We decided to char it under a hot grill (broiler) for a few minutes and it looked just like it had come out of a tandoor oven.

PREP TIME: 10 MINS,
PLUS MARINATING
COOKING TIME: HIGH
4–6 HRS

2.5kg (5lb 8oz) free-range
  chicken
Juice of 1–2 lemon, plus lemon
  wedges, to serve
1 tsp sea salt
3 tbsp melted butter,
  for basting (optional)

FOR THE MARINADE
4 tbsp plain Greek yogurt
2 tbsp Garlic and ginger paste
  (page 120)
3 green finger chillies,
  finely chopped
3 tbsp finely chopped
  coriander (cilantro)
2 tsp paprika
1 heaped tbsp Tandoori masala
  (page 119) or tandoori masala
  paste, or to taste

You can either remove the skin from the chicken here or leave it on. Score the chicken all over the breasts and thighs so that the marinade can get right into the meat. Place the chicken in a large mixing bowl and pour over the lime juice, then add the salt. Rub the lime juice and salt right into the flesh and in the cavity. Allow the chicken to rest while you prepare the marinade.

Whisk all the marinade ingredients together in a bowl until smooth, then rub the marinade all over the chicken, inside and out. You can leave it to marinate for up to 48 hours in the fridge or just go straight to cooking. The longer you can let the chicken marinate, the better.

When ready to cook, set your slow cooker to the high setting and place the chicken inside, breast-side up. Don't leave any of the marinade in the bowl – you want to rub it all into the meat and inside the bird. Slow cook for 4–6 hours with the lid on, being sure to check it after a couple of hours. The chicken is cooked when the internal temperature hits 74°C (164°F).

After 4–6 hours, the chicken will be cooked through and very juicy. This slow cooking method helps keep the meat moist. At this stage, you can simply tear or slice the meat off to serve it however you like, but I recommend heating your grill (broiler) as hot as you can get it and placing the chicken under it for a few minutes to char the exterior. If doing this, be sure to baste it generously with the melted butter before you place it in your oven, and then again during cooking. Serve with lemon wedges and/or a good raita.

LAMB RAAN

SERVES 4–6

The idea behind a good lamb raan is to slowly cook it until it is fall-apart tender. That applies however you cook it, so your slow cooker will make things easier and a lot less fussy. With other methods, you need to wrap the leg of lamb for cooking but that just isn't required in a slow cooker. Be sure to look for a lamb leg that will fit in your slow cooker and ask your butcher to break the bone at the end so that it isn't too long. After you marinate the meat, you can simply put it in your slow cooker and forget about it. Charring the cooked lamb leg in your oven at the end is optional for you but it's not optional for me – it's a must!

PREP TIME: 15 MINS, PLUS MARINATING
COOKING TIME: LOW 10 HRS

1 leg of lamb, surface fat removed
5 garlic cloves, cut into thin slivers
3 tbsp melted ghee, for basting

FOR THE MARINADE
1 red habanero chilli, plus extra if desired
5 tbsp crispy fried onions, homemade (page 51) or shop-bought
3 green bird's eye chillies, roughly chopped
1 tbsp ground cumin
1 tbsp ground coriander
1 tbsp Tandoori masala (page 119) or tandoori masala paste
1 tbsp Kashmiri chilli powder
1 tbsp freshly ground black pepper
1 tbsp sea salt, plus extra to taste
2 tbsp white wine vinegar
4 tbsp lemon juice
4 tbsp Garlic and ginger paste (page 120)
500g (2 cups) Greek yogurt

TO SERVE
Warm naans
Salad vegetables, such as shredded lettuce, tomato, cucumber and sliced onions

Place all the marinade ingredients except the yogurt in a food processor or blender. Then add 5 tablespoons of the yogurt and blend until you have a smooth, thick marinade. Whisk this into the remaining yogurt until creamy smooth. Set aside.

Make about eight deep slashes on each side of the leg of lamb; it should look mutilated, like roadkill! Take a sharp knife and make holes all over the meat, then stuff the garlic slivers into the holes. Now roll out a few large pieces of clingfilm (plastic wrap) and layer them in a baking dish. Place the lamb on top and pour the marinade over it. Rub the marinade all over the meat and into the slits.

Wrap the leg tightly with the clingfilm and allow to marinate in the fridge for at least 3 hours or up to 72 hours – the longer the better. If you are in a real rush, you could just go straight to cooking.

When ready to cook, place the leg of lamb and all the marinade in your slow cooker, cover and cook on the low setting for 10 hours. When your lamb raan is so tender you can literally tear the meat from the bone, it's ready, but charring the raan will make it even better.

This step is optional. Preheat your oven to its highest temperature and place the raan in a roasting pan. Baste it with the ghee and set it inside to roast for about 20 minutes. While the lamb is roasting, pour the juices from your slow cooker into a small pan and heat them to a simmer.

With the raan charred to your liking, place it on a serving platter and take your masterpiece to the table. Serve it with the heated sauce and any side dishes that sound good. I like this simply with warm naans and cold salad vegetables.

CHANA MASALA

SERVES 4

When cooking a chana masala, the chickpeas are the star ingredient. For this reason, I always cook my chickpeas from dry as they are better than tinned (canned) and you get the added bonus of being able to use the cooking liquid in your sauce. You can use tinned chickpeas for ease though. The sauce can be made the way I prefer it – blended and smooth – or you could leave it chunky, if you like.

PREP TIME: 10 MINS
COOKING TIME: HIGH 2¼ HRS, LOW 4–6 HRS

2 tbsp rapeseed (canola) oil
1 tsp cumin seeds
2.5cm (1in) real cinnamon stick
3 cloves
3 green cardamom pods, lightly bruised
2 onions, finely chopped
2 tbsp Garlic and ginger paste (page 120)
2 green finger chillies, roughly chopped
½ tsp ground turmeric
1 tsp Garam masala (page 119)
1 tsp chaat masala (optional)
2 tsp Kashmiri chilli powder
2 tsp ground coriander
2 tsp ground cumin
½ tsp amchoor (dried mango powder)
200g (7oz) tinned (canned) chopped tomatoes
80ml (⅓ cup) water or chickpea broth
500g (3 cups) cooked chickpeas (garbanzos), tinned (canned) or slow cooked (see right)
1 tsp kasoori methi (dried fenugreek leaves)
Sea salt, to taste
3 tbsp finely chopped coriander (cilantro)

TO SERVE
Lemon wedges
Naans, chapatis or parathas

Heat the oil in your slow cooker using the sauté/searing mode or in a pan over a medium–high heat. When the oil begins to lightly sizzle, add in the cumin seeds, cinnamon stick, cloves and cardamom pods and fry for about 30 seconds, stirring frequently, to release their flavour into the oil.

Stir in the chopped onions and fry for about 5 minutes, until soft and translucent. Add the garlic and ginger paste and chillies. Fry for another minute or so, stirring regularly. Stir in the turmeric, garam masala, chaat masala, chilli powder, ground coriander, cumin and amchoor and continue sautéing and stirring for another minute.

Add the chopped tomatoes and the water or broth and bring to a simmer. At this stage you can either blend everything until smooth or you can leave it all as is for a chunkier sauce. Add the chickpeas and cook on the high setting for 2 hours or low for 4–6 hours. When the curry is ready, the chickpeas will be almost falling apart.

Add the kasoori methi by rubbing it between your fingers over the chana masala. Season with salt to taste and garnish with the chopped coriander. I like to serve this with lemon wedges that can be squeezed over the curry to taste at the table. Serve with naans, chapatis or parathas that can be used to scoop it all up.

*TIP

If you would like to cook dried chickpeas for this recipe in your slow cooker, it's really easy. This will make enough for 2 chana masala curries or you could use the leftovers for other things. The cooked chickpeas freeze well too.

Wash 350g (2 cups) dried chickpeas thoroughly and pick out any stones if you see any before cooking. Pour the washed chickpeas into your slow cooker and cover with about 7.5cm (3in) of water. You can always add a little boiling water if needed later in cooking.

Cover with the lid and cook on the high setting for 6–10 hours depending on how you are using the chickpeas. For most curries, you can cook them until they are about as tender as tinned chickpeas, which will take about 6–7 hours. If you are using them in a hummus, you can nuke them for 10 hours.

RAJMA

SERVES 4

One of the best rajmas I ever tried was in Rajasthan where the kidney beans were cooked so long they were falling apart, making an incredibly creamy and tasty sauce. You can only get that using dried kidney beans. I know – I tried with tinned (canned) beans. Dried kidney beans take some preparation, though, as they can be toxic if under-cooked, so you need to soak and boil them first. After that, you'll find slow cooking a rajma might just be the best way to cook it. For best results, slow cook this on low for 10 hours and don't be tempted to speed things up by cooking on the high setting. If you want to make things easy on yourself, use 3 x 400g (14oz) tins or about 3 cups of kidney beans. Only add 175ml (¾ cup) water and cook on high for 2 hours or low for 4 hours.

300g (1½ cups) dried red kidney beans, soaked for 8 hours
3 tbsp rapeseed (canola) oil or ghee
1 tsp cumin seeds
3 onions, roughly chopped
1 tbsp Garlic and ginger paste (page 120)
2 green finger chillies, finely chopped
1½ tsp Kashmiri chilli powder, or to taste
½ tsp ground turmeric
1½ tsp ground cumin
1½ tsp ground coriander
2 tsp tomato paste
125ml (½ cup) unseasoned passata
1 tsp kasoori methi (dried fenugreek leaves)
¼ tsp Garam masala (page 119)
Sea salt, to taste
3 tbsp chopped fresh coriander (cilantro), to garnish

Bring a large pan of water to the boil. Drain the soaked kidney beans and wash them thoroughly under cold water. Pour the beans into the boiling water and boil vigorously for 20 minutes, then strain them and set aside.

Heat the oil in a slow cooker using the sauté/searing mode or in a pan over a medium heat. When visibly hot, add the cumin seeds and stir them into the oil for about 30 seconds. Add the chopped onions and fry for about 8 minutes, or until golden brown. Stir in the garlic and ginger paste along with the chopped chillies.

Now add the Kashmiri chilli powder, turmeric, cumin and ground coriander and stir these spices into the onion mixture. Add the tomato paste and passata and continue simmering until oil bubbles separate and rise to the top. Allow to cool a little and then blend to a smooth and medium-thick sauce using a stick or countertop blender.

Add the sauce, the beans and 1 litre (4 cups) of boiling water to your slow cooker. Cook on low for 10 hours.

To finish, add the kasoori methi to the sauce by rubbing between your fingers. Stir it in and season with salt to taste. Sprinkle the garam masala over the top and whisk it some to make your rajma good and creamy. Garnish with the chopped coriander to serve.

*NOTE

If you find that the rajma is too soupy, you can cook it down using the sauté/searing function on your slow cooker with the lid off or in a pot over a high heat on the stove. If it is too thick, stir in a little water.

SAAG CURRY

SERVES 4

Saag is one of the most popular vegetarian curries. It can be served simply over white rice. It also can be added either in small or large amounts to other curries. If you like spinach, this is really good stirred into any lamb or chicken curry. You might also like to make this into a saag paneer by adding cubed paneer to heat through during the last hour of cooking, which is what I did in the photo opposite. You could make this curry just with spinach but the additional greens do give it more character.

**PREP TIME: 15 MINS
COOKING TIME: HIGH 3
HRS, LOW 6 HRS**

240g (9oz) spinach leaves
2 bunches (about 150g/5oz)
  of mustard leaves, chopped
½ bunch (about 80g/3oz)
  of fresh fenugreek leaves,
  chopped
2 tbsp rapeseed (canola) oil
1 tsp cumin seeds
1 white onion, roughly chopped
6 garlic cloves, roughly chopped
2.5cm (1in) piece of root ginger,
  roughly chopped
2–3 green finger chillies
2 tomatoes, diced
2 tsp ground coriander
1½ tsp ground cumin
½ tsp Kashmiri chilli powder,
  or to taste
¼ tsp ground turmeric
1 tbsp fine cornmeal flour
Sea salt, to taste
2 tbsp butter or ghee
70ml (¼ cup) single (light)
  cream (optional)
White rice, to serve

Prepare all the greens by washing thoroughly under cold running water to remove any dirt or sand. Set aside. Bring a large pan of water to the boil and blanch the greens for 30 seconds, working in small batches. Using a slotted spoon, transfer to a bowl to cool, then squeeze out the excess moisture into a bowl. Reserve 300ml (1¼ cups) of the liquid as you will need it later. Roughly chop all these greens and set aside.

Heat the oil in your slow cooker using the sauté/searing mode or in a frying pan over a medium–high heat. When the oil begins to shimmer, stir in the cumin seeds and let their flavour infuse into the oil for about 30 seconds. Then add the chopped onion and fry for about 3 minutes or until softened. Add the garlic, ginger and chillies and continue frying for another 1–2 minutes. Stir in the tomatoes and the ground spices. This is your base masala.

Add the blanched greens to your slow cooker along with the base masala and the 300ml (1¼ cups) of reserved water, then cook on the high setting for 2 hours or low for 4 hours. Whisk in the cornmeal flour and continue cooking for another hour on the high setting or 2 hours on low.

To finish, season with salt to taste and add the butter or ghee to melt into the saag. If you like, you can make it nice and creamy by stirring in the cream and/or swirling it over as a garnish.

ALOO GOBI

SERVES 4

Aloo gobi, or potato and cauliflower curry, is the perfect dish for slow cooking. As the potatoes and cauliflower gently cook, they release moisture which becomes part of the finished sauce. Remember, no one likes a hard potato. Cooking times may vary so check the curry before serving and cook it a little longer if the potatoes are not tender.

PREP TIME: 15 MINS
COOKING TIME: HIGH 3 HRS, LOW 6 HRS

350g (12oz) russet potatoes
350g (12oz) cauliflower
2–3 tbsp rapeseed (canola) oil
1 tsp black mustard seeds
1 tsp cumin seeds
1 onion, very finely chopped
3–4 green bird's eye chillies, finely chopped
2 tbsp Garlic and ginger paste (page 120)
1 tbsp Mixed powder or Curry powder (page 118)
1 tsp ground turmeric
1 tsp amchoor (dried mango powder)
2 tsp Kashmiri chilli powder, or to taste
200g (7oz) chopped tomatoes
Sea salt, to taste
3 tbsp chopped coriander (cilantro), to garnish

Peel and cut the potatoes into 5cm (2in) chunks and chop the cauliflower into pieces that are just slightly larger than the potatoes. Set aside.

Heat the oil in your slow cooker using the sauté/searing mode or in a frying pan over a medium–high heat. When the oil begins to shimmer from the heat, add the mustard seeds. When they begin to crackle, add the cumin seeds and let these spices infuse into the oil for about 30 seconds.

Stir in the chopped onion and chillies and sauté for about 5 minutes, or until the onion is soft and translucent. Add the garlic and ginger paste and stir well. You want to cook this for about 30 seconds to cook out the rawness, then add the ground spices and chopped tomatoes.

Bring this all to a simmer, then add the potatoes and cauliflower. Stir well so that the potatoes and cauliflower are completely coated with the other ingredients and then cook it all in your slow cooker, covered with the lid, on the high setting for 3 hours or low for 6 hours. Cooking times may vary so do check it – the curry is ready when you are happy with the doneness of the potatoes and cauliflower.

When cooked to your liking, season with salt to taste and serve garnished with the chopped coriander.

BROCCOLI AND/OR CAULIFLOWER CURRY

SERVES 4

You can use broccoli, cauliflower or a combination of both for this easy curry. Either way, the flavours are amazing. I prefer to use both. If you are able to watch the curry as it cooks, you can simply fry off the onions, garlic and ginger and the spices and then add the broccoli and/or cauliflower and let it cook until the vegetables are cooked to your preferred doneness. If you are not able to keep an eye on it all, I recommend steaming the broccoli and/or cauliflower until tender and then adding them to the sauce at the end of cooking.

PREP TIME: 15 MINS
COOKING TIME: HIGH 3¼
HRS, LOW 6 HRS

625g (1lb 6oz) broccoli
  and/or cauliflower
3 tbsp coconut oil
70g (2½oz) grated fresh or
  frozen coconut
1 onion, finely chopped
½ tsp sea salt
2 tbsp Garlic and ginger paste
  (page 120)
3 green finger chillies,
  finely chopped
3 tomatoes, diced
1 tsp Kashmiri chilli powder,
  or to taste
1 tsp turmeric
300ml (1¼ cups) thick
  coconut milk
1 handful of roasted cashews,
  roughly chopped (optional)
3 tbsp toasted sesame seeds
Sea salt and freshly ground
  black pepper
3 tbsp finely chopped coriander
  (cilantro) leaves, to garnish

If you are cooking the broccoli and/or cauliflower separately, bring about 5cm (2in) of water to the boil and steam the broccoli and/or cauliflower florets until just cooked through. Set aside. If you are cooking the vegetables with the other ingredients, you can skip this step.

Heat a tablespoon of the oil in your slow cooker using the sauté/sear function or in a pan over a high heat. When the oil begins to shimmer, add the grated coconut and fry it for a couple of minutes, stirring regularly, until it turns light golden brown. Using a slotted spoon, transfer to a plate and set aside.

Now heat the remaining oil in the cooker or pan and add the chopped onion and salt. Fry for about 5 minutes, stirring frequently, or until soft and translucent. Add the garlic and ginger paste and the chillies and fry for a further 30 seconds. Then stir in the diced tomatoes, chilli powder and turmeric.

If you are cooking the broccoli and/or cauliflower in the sauce, add them now along with the coconut milk and stir well to combine.

In your slow cooker, cover these ingredients with the lid and cook on the high setting for 3 hours or low for 6 hours. Remember that not all slow cookers are the same so if you are cooking the vegetables at the same time, check them from time to time so that they don't overcook and become mushy. When the vegetables are cooked to your liking, stir in the chopped cashews, if using, the browned coconut and the toasted sesame seeds. Season with salt and pepper to taste and serve garnished with the chopped coriander.

BOMBAY ALOO

SERVES 4

I normally serve Bombay potatoes as a side dish but they also make a good vegetarian main dish. If doing this, they are good served with Tarka dal (page 76).

PREP TIME: 15 MINS
COOKING TIME: HIGH 3¼
HRS, LOW 4–6 HRS

3 tbsp rapeseed (canola) oil
1 tsp black mustard seeds
½ tsp fenugreek seeds
3 dried red Kashmiri chillies
2 onions, thinly sliced and cut
  into 2.5cm (1in) pieces
½ tsp sea salt, plus extra
  to taste
2 tbsp Garlic and ginger paste
  (page 120)
5 green finger chillies: 2 finely
  chopped, plus 3 left whole
2 tsp Curry powder (page 118)
1–2 tsp Kashmiri chilli powder
1 tsp ground cumin
1 tsp ground coriander
1kg (lb 4oz) new potatoes,
  cut in half
400ml (14oz) tinned (canned)
  chopped tomatoes
1 tsp tamarind concentrate
½ tsp Garam masala (page 119)
1 tsp kasoori methi (dried
  fenugreek leaves)
Freshly ground black pepper,
  to taste
3 tbsp finely chopped coriander
  (cilantro) leaves, to garnish
2 limes, quartered

Heat the oil in your slow cooker using the sauté/searing function or in a pan over a medium–high heat. When the oil is visibly hot, stir in the mustard seeds, then, when they begin to crackle from the heat, stir in the fenugreek seeds and dried Kashmiri chillies and stir them around for about 30 seconds.

Stir in the sliced onions, sprinkle with the salt and fry for about 5 minutes, or until soft and translucent. Then stir in the garlic and ginger paste and the finely chopped chillies, followed by the curry powder, chilli powder, cumin and ground coriander. Add the new potatoes, chopped tomatoes and tamarind concentrate.

In your slow cooker with the lid on, cook on the high setting for 3 hours or low for 4–6 hours. Your Bombay potatoes are ready to serve when the potatoes are deliciously soft, so don't rush things! Stir in the garam masala, and the kasoori methi by rubbing it between your fingers over the sauce. Then add the whole chillies and stir them into the sauce too.

To finish, season with salt and pepper to taste, garnish with the chopped coriander and serve with the lime wedges, which can be squeezed over the top at the table.

TARKA DAL

SERVES 4

This is one where you really could just throw all the ingredients in your slow cooker to cook and it will still come out tasting like a good dal. I don't recommend doing that though. Slow cook the lentils and then take a couple of minutes at the end to fry the tarka ingredients in a pan before pouring it all over the hot lentils and stirring it in. That is the flavour you want!

PREP TIME: 10 MINS, PLUS SOAKING TIME COOKING TIME: HIGH 3 HRS, LOW 6+ HRS

300g (10½oz) masoor dal (red lentils), rinsed
750ml (3 cups) water or vegetable stock, plus extra if needed
4 tbsp ghee
1 tsp black mustard seeds
1 tsp cumin seeds
10 fresh or frozen curry leaves
1 onion, thinly sliced and cut into small pieces
3 garlic cloves, finely chopped (minced)
1 tsp Kashmiri chilli powder, or to taste
1 tbsp Garam masala (page 119)
½ tsp ground turmeric
Sea salt and freshly ground black pepper, to taste

Rinse the lentils and then pour them into your slow cooker. Cover with the water or stock, ensuring that they are completely submerged. If not, add a little more water so that the lentils are covered by at least 1cm (½in) of water.

Slow cook, with the lid on, on the high setting for 3 hours or low for 6 hours or even longer. You can let these lentils stew overnight if you like!

When the lentils are cooked through and really soft, you could mash them with a potato masher, blend them until creamy smooth with a hand-blender or just leave them as they are. If it is too thick, you could add a drop more water or stock.

To make the tarka, heat the ghee in a frying pan over a medium–high heat. When it is bubbling hot, add the mustard seeds, and when they begin to crackle, stir in the cumin seeds and curry leaves and let them fry for about 30 seconds. Add the onion and garlic and fry for a further 3 minutes over a medium heat. Stir in the chilli powder, garam masala and turmeric and fry for a further 30 seconds.

Pour most of this tarka over the lentils and stir it in, reserving a little to add at the end as a garnish. Season the lentils with salt and pepper to taste, then pour the remaining tarka over the top to serve.

CHANA DAL

Just like the Tarka dal on page 76, you will get good results if you just throw all the ingredients in your slow cooker and let it cook. You will like it even more, though, if you take a couple of minutes to make the tarka and add it right before serving. Chana dal is my favourite dal, especially when blended until creamy smooth.

PREP TIME: 10 MINS, PLUS SOAKING TIME
COOKING TIME: HIGH 2¼ HRS, LOW 4¼ HRS

300g (10½oz) chana lentils, rinsed and soaked in water for 30 minutes
750ml (3 cups) water or hot vegetable stock
4 tbsp ghee
½ tsp black mustard seeds
1 tsp cumin seeds
Pinch of asafoetida*
1 tsp ground turmeric
½ onion, finely chopped
5 garlic cloves, cut into slivers
1 tbsp Garlic and ginger paste (page 120)
1–5 fresh green finger chillies, finely chopped (to taste)
3 tomatoes, roughly chopped
½ tsp ground cumin
½ tbsp ground coriander
½ tsp Garam masala (page 119)
Sea salt, to taste
Chopped coriander (cilantro), to garnish

Place the lentils in your slow cooker and top with the boiling water or hot stock. Cook, with the lid on, on the high setting for 2 hours or 4 hours on low.

When the dal is cooked to perfection, make the tarka. Melt the ghee in a pan over a high heat. When it is visibly very hot, add the mustard seeds. They will begin to pop after about 30 seconds. Reduce the heat to medium–high and add the cumin seeds and asafoetida. Temper in the ghee for about 30 seconds, then add the turmeric and chopped onion and fry until soft and translucent – 3–5 minutes should do the job. Stir in the slivered garlic, the garlic and ginger paste and the chillies, and cook, stirring continuously, for another 30 seconds. Then stir in the tomatoes, ground cumin, ground coriander and garam masala. Take off the heat but keep warm.

To serve, you can either leave the dal as it is, smash it with a potato masher or blend it until smooth with a hand-held blender or just whisk it lightly. I prefer it blended. Season the dal with salt to taste and then pour the contents of the pan over the dal, stirring some of it right in while leaving some floating on top. Garnish with the chopped coriander to serve.

*NOTE

If you are gluten-free, please check the asafoetida packaging, as some brands contain wheat flour.

DAL MAKHANI
SERVES 4, OR MORE AS PART OF A MULTI-COURSE MEAL

Dal makhani isn't a dal you can rush, as these lentils need a good long cook – so this recipe is perfect for the slow cooker. In fact, I think they are better if you cook on low for 8–10 hours rather than trying to speed things up by cooking on the high setting. So some forward planning might be a good idea. I usually soak the lentils all day on day one, then place them in the slow cooker overnight. Once they are cooked, this is a quick and easy dish.

PREP TIME: 10 MINS,
PLUS SOAKING TIME
COOKING TIME: LOW
8–10 HRS

300g (10½oz) black urad
   dal, soaked overnight
   in cold water
750ml (3 cups) boiling water,
   plus extra if needed
5 tbsp rapeseed (canola) oil
2 onions, finely chopped
2 tbsp Garlic and ginger paste
   (page 120)
2 tomatoes, diced
2 tsp Kashmiri chilli powder
1 tsp ground turmeric
1 tbsp Garam masala (page 119)
1 tsp paprika
250ml (1 cup) single
   (light) cream
2 tsp sea salt, or to taste
3 tbsp butter, or to taste
4 tbsp chopped coriander
   (cilantro) leaves, to garnish

For best results, rinse and then soak the urad lentils for 8 hours. Rinsing is required but you could get away with not soaking them. It might just take longer for them to cook.

Place the lentils in your slow cooker, pour in the water and cook on low for 8 hours. Sometime during the day, when it is convenient, heat the oil in a frying pan over a medium–high heat and add the chopped onions. Fry for 10 minutes, or until the onions are soft, translucent and lightly browned and then add the garlic and ginger paste and fry for a further minute. Turn off the heat and stir in the tomatoes, chilli powder, turmeric, garam masala and paprika. Stir for a minute into the hot oil, then set aside.

Check the lentils after 8 hours to ensure they are fall-apart soft. If not, continue cooking. Once soft, mash them with a potato masher or blend using a stick blender.

Pour in the prepared onion and spice mixture. You want the dal makhani to be good and hot, so if serving later you could reheat it using the sauté/searing mode of your slow cooker or in a pot on your stove.

Just before serving, stir in most of the cream and season with salt to taste. Top with the butter, which will melt into the dal. I usually swirl a little cream on top at the end before garnishing with the chopped coriander.

MORE CURRIES, STEWS AND SOUPS OF THE WORLD

In this section I have included some of the most
popular curries, stews and soups from South
East Asia. Remember that, for ease, you could just
throw all the ingredients in your slow cooker and
cook them while you get on with your day.
I highly recommend following the recipes as
written though. Frying the different ingredients
will achieve a more authentic-tasting dish.

THAI GREEN CHICKEN CURRY
SERVES 4

Thai curries work so well in a slow cooker. They are usually soupier than Indian curries but you still only need to add 400ml (1¾ cups) of coconut milk for the liquid. As the chicken slowly cooks, it releases more liquid. You will have the perfect amount of sauce to pour over the rice. For ease, you can substitute 2–3 tablespoons of shop-bought green curry paste if you don't want to make your own. Start with 2 tablespoons and then add more if needed at the end of cooking. Needless to say, if you make your own paste, your curry will be better!

**PREP TIME: 15 MINS
COOKING TIME: HIGH 3¼
HRS, LOW 6¼ HRS**

3 tbsp coconut or rapeseed (canola) oil
700g (1lb 9oz) chicken thighs or breasts, cut into bite-sized pieces (and seared in the hot oil (page 6) if you wish)
400ml (1¾ cups) coconut milk
10 baby sweetcorn, cut into small pieces
1 handful of mangetout (snow peas), cut diagonally into thirds
1–2 tbsp Thai fish sauce*

FOR THE CURRY PASTE
1 tsp cumin seeds
1 tsp coriander seeds
1½ tsp white pepper
15 green bird's eye chillies, roughly chopped, or to taste
8 garlic cloves, smashed
3 small shallots, roughly chopped
1 tbsp finely chopped Thai sweet basil stalks (about 10)
½ tbsp finely chopped coriander (cilantro) stalks (about 5)
1 thumb-sized piece of galangal, thinly sliced
Zest of ½ lime
5 makrut lime leaves, fresh or frozen
2 lemongrass stalks, finely chopped (about 4 generous tbsp)
1 tsp shrimp paste

Optional but for best results, heat a frying pan over a medium heat and toast the cumin and coriander seeds until warm to the touch and fragrant but not yet smoking. Transfer to a pestle and mortar and then pound into a fine powder. Transfer this powder to a plate and add the white pepper. Set aside. If time is an issue, you could just add half a teaspoon each of ground cumin and coriander.

Put the remaining curry paste ingredients into a blender or food processor and pour in the toasted cumin, coriander and white pepper powder. Blend to a smooth, thick paste, adding just enough water to do so. Some blenders will require more water for blending but try to keep it to a minimum, adding a spoonful at a time and remembering that the paste needs to be thick, not runny.

Now heat the oil in a frying pan over a medium–high heat or set your slow cooker to sear if you have a sauté/searing mode. Add the green curry paste and fry it for a couple of minutes, stirring continuously. Stir in the chicken, coconut milk, baby sweetcorn and mangetout and bring to a simmer.

In your slow cooker, cook, with the lid on, on the high setting for 3 hours or low for 6 hours. When the curry is ready, stir in a tablespoon of fish sauce. Try it and add more fish sauce or salt to taste, if needed. Serve over jasmine rice or rice noodles.

*NOTE
Some Thai fish sauces contain gluten, but there are gluten-free brands available.

THAI RED CHICKEN CURRY

SERVES 4

Many people think that red Thai curry is the spiciest because it's red but it's not – green curry is. If you like a good spicy curry, you won't be disappointed, though, and you could always add more chillies at the end to give it a kick, but I doubt you'll need to do that.

PREP TIME: 15 MINS
COOKING TIME: HIGH 3¼ HRS, LOW 6¼ HRS

2 tbsp coconut oil or rapeseed (canola) oil
450g (1lb) skinless chicken thighs, cut into bite-sized pieces (and seared in the hot oil (page 6) if you wish)
400ml (1¾ cups) thick coconut milk
About 225g (8oz) vegetables, such as baby sweetcorn, broccoli or green beans
1 tbsp light soy sauce* or tamari (GF)
1 tsp tamarind concentrate
1 tbsp palm sugar
1–2 tbsp fish sauce
Coriander (cilantro) leaves, to garnish

FOR THE CURRY PASTE
1 tbsp cumin seeds
1 tbsp coriander seeds
1½ tsp white pepper
12 dried red bird's eye chillies, soaked in water for 30 minutes, then cut into small pieces
12 garlic cloves, roughly chopped
2 medium shallots, finely chopped
1 thumb-sized piece of galangal, thinly sliced
2 red spur chillies, thinly sliced
1 lemongrass stalk, tough outer part removed, stalk thinly sliced
10 thick coriander stalks (about 1 generous tbsp), finely chopped
Zest of ½ lime
1 tsp shrimp paste

Optional but for best results, toast the cumin and coriander seeds in a dry frying pan over a medium heat until fragrant and warm to the touch but not yet smoking. Transfer to a pestle and mortar and then pound into a fine powder. Transfer this powder to a plate and add the white pepper. Set aside. If time is an issue, you could just add half a teaspoon each of ground cumin and ground coriander.

Put the remaining curry paste ingredients into a blender or food processor and pour in the toasted cumin, coriander and white pepper powder. Blend to a smooth, thick paste, adding just enough water to do so. Some blenders will require more water for blending but try to keep it to a minimum, adding a spoonful at a time and remembering that the paste needs to be thick, not runny.

Now heat the oil in a frying pan over a medium–high heat or set your slow cooker to sear if you have a sauté/searing mode. Add the red curry paste and fry it for a couple of minutes, stirring continuously. Stir in the chicken, coconut milk and your veggies of choice and bring to a simmer. For best results, you could steam vegetables like broccoli and green beans – as you will have more control over their doneness – but you can add them now if you like. If you steam them, add them just before serving.

In your slow cooker, stir all the ingredients well, including the soy sauce, tamarind concentrate and sugar, then cover with the lid and cook for 3 hours on the high setting or 6 hours on low.

Stir in 1–2 tablespoons of fish sauce. Taste it and add more fish sauce or salt to taste. Serve over jasmine rice or rice noodles. Serving garnished with chopped coriander and Chinese crispy chilli oil is very nice.

*NOTE
Many soy sauces contain gluten, but there are gluten-free brands available.

THAI YELLOW CURRY
SERVES 4

Like massaman curry, Thai yellow curry definitely has Indian influences: the yellow colour comes from the turmeric in the curry paste as well as the curry powder, which is also used. Many people liken this curry to an Indian restaurant-style chicken korma because it is yellow and made with coconut but it is normally a bit spicier than a korma.

PREP TIME: 15 MINS
COOKING TIME: HIGH 3¼
HRS, LOW 6–8 HRS

2 tbsp rapeseed (canola) oil
700g (1lb 7oz) skinless chicken
   thighs, cut into bite-sized
   pieces (and seared (page 6)
   if you wish)
400ml (1¾ cups) thick
   coconut milk
1 tbsp palm or white sugar
1 tbsp tamarind concentrate
1 tsp Curry powder (page 118)
10 small waxy new potatoes,
   quartered
1 carrot, cut into thin rounds
2 tbsp Thai fish sauce*
10 baby plum tomatoes, halved
Chopped chillies, to garnish
4 tbsp fried garlic slivers,
   to garnish (optional)

FOR THE CURRY PASTE
1½ tsp cumin seeds
1½ tsp coriander seeds
½ tsp green cardamom seeds
   (optional)
1½ tsp white pepper
12 dried red bird's eye chillies,
   soaked in water for 30 minutes
   then finely chopped
12 garlic cloves
1 thumb-sized piece of galangal,
   peeled and thinly sliced
1 thumb-sized piece of fresh
   turmeric, peeled and thinly
   sliced, or 1–1½ tsp ground
3 lime leaves, stalks removed
   and finely chopped
3 medium shallots, halved
10 thick coriander stalks
½ lemongrass stalk, tough outer
   part removed, stalk sliced
1 tsp shrimp paste

Optional but for best results, toast the cumin seeds, coriander seeds and cardamom seeds, if using, in a dry frying pan over a medium heat until fragrant and warm to the touch but not yet smoking. Transfer to a pestle and mortar to cool a little and then pound into a fine powder. Transfer this powder to a plate and add the white pepper. Set aside. If time is an issue, you could just add ½ teaspoon each of ground cumin and coriander.

Put the remaining curry paste ingredients into a blender or food processor and pour in the toasted cumin, coriander and white pepper powder. Blend to a smooth, thick paste, adding just enough water to do so. Some blenders will require more water for blending but try to keep it to a minimum, adding a spoonful at a time and remembering that the paste needs to be thick, not runny.

Now heat the oil in a frying pan over a medium–high heat or set your slow cooker to sear if you have a sauté/searing mode. Add the yellow curry paste and fry it for a couple of minutes, stirring continuously. Stir in the chicken, coconut milk, sugar, tamarind concentrate, curry powder, potatoes and carrots. If you would like a bit of bite to your carrots, I recommend holding them back and steaming them separately and then adding them to the sauce just before serving, but you can add them now if you like, for ease.

Cover and cook in your slow cooker for 3 hours on the high setting or 6–8 hours on low.

About 10 minutes before the curry is ready, stir in a tablespoon of the fish sauce. Try the curry and add another tablespoon of fish sauce or salt, if needed, to taste. Add the tomatoes to heat through and serve over jasmine rice or rice noodles. This curry is nice garnished with chopped chillies and fried garlic slivers.

*NOTE
Some Thai fish sauces contain gluten, but there are gluten-free brands available.

BEEF PANANG
SERVES 4

Panang curry paste is a lot like a red curry but slightly milder and usually sweeter, plus it has the delicious addition of roasted peanuts. Of course, you can make your panang curry paste as spicy or sweet as you like. Shop-bought panang curry pastes often don't include peanuts for allergy reasons, but peanuts are a key ingredient, so as long as you aren't intolerant, they must go in! If you want to use a shop-bought curry paste, start with about 3 tablespoons. You can always add more. For best results, I recommend steaming or stir-frying the vegetables so that you can cook them to your preferred doneness, but you can just slow cook them with everything else if you like.

PREP TIME: 15 MINS
COOKING TIME: HIGH 4¼
HRS, LOW 6–8 HRS

700g (1lb 7oz) stewing beef
2 tbsp rapeseed (canola) oil
400ml (1¾ cups) thick
    coconut milk
1–2 tbsp palm sugar
About 225g (8oz) vegetables,
    such as chopped baby
    sweetcorn, courgette
    (zucchini), mushrooms
2 tbsp Thai fish sauce*, to taste

FOR THE CURRY PASTE
1 tbsp cumin seeds
1 tbsp coriander seeds
1½ tsp white pepper
12 dried red bird's eye chillies,
    soaked in water for 30 minutes
    then finely chopped
12 garlic cloves, roughly chopped
2 shallots, finely chopped
1 thumb-sized piece of galangal,
    peeled and thinly sliced
2 fresh red chillies, thinly sliced
1 lemongrass stalk, tough outer
    part removed, stalk sliced
10 thick coriander (cilantro) stalks
Zest of ½ lime
4 makrut lime leaves, stems
    removed and finely chopped
3–4 tbsp roasted peanuts
1 tsp shrimp paste

TO SERVE
3 lime leaves, stalks removed
3 tbsp roasted peanuts
Jasmine rice or rice noodles

Optional but for best results, toast the cumin and coriander seeds in a dry frying pan over a medium heat until fragrant and warm to the touch but not yet smoking. Transfer to a pestle and mortar to cool a little and then pound into a fine powder. Transfer this powder to a plate and add the white pepper. Set aside. If time is an issue, you could just add half a teaspoon each of ground cumin and coriander.

Put the remaining curry paste ingredients into a blender or food processor and pour in the toasted cumin, coriander and white pepper powder. Blend to a smooth, thick paste, adding just enough water to do so. Some blenders will require more water for blending but try to keep it to a minimum, adding a spoonful at a time and remembering that the paste needs to be thick, not runny.

Now prepare the beef by cutting it thinly against the grain. Heat the oil in a frying pan over a medium–high heat or set your slow cooker to sear if you have a sauté/searing mode. Add the panang curry paste and fry it for a couple of minutes, stirring continuously. Stir in the beef, coconut milk, sugar and your veggies of choice and bring to a simmer. For best results, I recommend steaming your vegetables separately so that you have more control over their doneness, but you can add them now if you like. If you steam them, add them just before serving.

In your slow cooker, cook with the lid on for 4 hours on the high setting or 6–8 hours on low.

When the beef is tender, stir in 1–2 tablespoons of fish sauce, or to taste. Finely julienne the lime leaves and roughly chop the peanuts, if using. Serve the panang over jasmine rice or rice noodles, garnished with the lime leaves and the peanuts.

*NOTE
Some Thai fish sauces contain gluten, but there are gluten-free brands available.

PORK JUNGLE CURRY
SERVES 4

Normally, I don't recommend using a shop-bought curry paste but it does work in this recipe. You could, of course, use a batch of homemade red curry paste (page 86) if you like. Jungle curry is a spicy one and it's different to other Thai curries as there is no coconut milk in it. For this reason, it can taste spicier and is more soupy than others. It's one of my favourite Thai curries!

PREP TIME: 15 MINS
COOKING TIME: HIGH 4¼
HRS, LOW 6–8 HRS

2 tbsp rapeseed (canola), peanut or coconut oil

6 tbsp Thai red curry paste, shop-bought or homemade (page 86), plus extra if needed

1kg (2lb 4oz) pork shoulder, cut into bite-sized pieces (and seared in the hot oil (page 6) if you wish)

300ml (1¼ cups) unsalted shop-bought or homemade chicken stock (page 117) or water

10 green beans, cut into 2.5cm (1in) pieces

227g (8oz) tin of bamboo shoots, drained and cut into matchsticks

5 baby sweetcorn, cut into small pieces

3 tbsp fresh green peppercorns (optional)

6 lime leaves, stalks removed and leaves thinly sliced

Juice of ½ lime

1 tsp palm sugar (optional)

TO SERVE

4 tbsp coriander (cilantro) leaves

2–3 tbsp Thai fish sauce*

1 small bunch of Thai sweet basil leaves

Rice

Set your slow cooker to sauté/searing mode if you have that function or heat a pan over a medium–high heat. Add the oil and, when it begins to glisten, add the curry paste and fry it for about 2 minutes to cook out the rawness. Add the remaining ingredients up to and including the sugar and stir well to combine.

Cover with the lid and slow cook on the high setting for 4 hours or low for 6–8 hours. The curry is ready when the pork is tender.

To finish, stir in the fresh coriander. Add 2 tablespoons of fish sauce and try it. If needed, add a little more fish sauce or salt to taste. As I mentioned above, this is a spicy curry so feel free to add more red curry paste if you like.

Garnish with the sweet basil leaves and serve over rice.

*NOTE

Many Thai fish sauces contain gluten, but there are gluten-free brands available.

BEEF MASSAMAN CURRY

SERVES 4

Beef Massaman curry is believed to have been brought to Thailand by Persian and Indian sea merchants, and judging from the spices used, it most likely was. Back then, the Muslim cooks of this curry found it difficult to find halal beef so it was usually made with chicken. Nowadays, beef Massaman is much more popular. I hope you make the Massaman curry paste and sear the meat, as per the recipe, but if you want to make things easier on yourself, you could just use 3–4 tablespoons of shop-bought Massaman paste and top it up at the end of cooking, if needed.

PREP TIME: 15 MINS
COOKING TIME: HIGH 4¼ HRS, LOW 6–8 HRS

2 tbsp rapeseed (canola) oil
700g (1lb 9oz) stewing beef, cut into bite-sized pieces
2 potatoes, peeled and cut into bite-sized pieces
½ red onion, quartered
400ml (2 cups) thick coconut milk
1 tbsp palm sugar
1 tsp tamarind concentrate
1 handful of roasted peanuts
3 tbsp Thai fish sauce*
Sea salt, to taste
Thai holy basil, to garnish

FOR THE CURRY PASTE

1 tbsp coriander seeds
1½ tbsp cumin seeds
5 whole cloves
1 tbsp black peppercorns
Seeds from 6 green cardamom pods
5cm (2in) real cinnamon stick
1 whole nutmeg, smashed into small pieces
12 dried red bird's eye chillies, soaked in water for 30 minutes, then finely chopped
8 garlic cloves, smashed
2–3 small shallots, thinly sliced
1 long lemongrass stalk, outer tough parts removed, stalk thinly sliced
1 thumb-sized piece of galangal, sliced into thin rounds
Zest of ½ lime
3 lime leaves (fresh or frozen)
1 tsp shrimp paste

Optional but for best results, toast the coriander seeds, cumin seeds, cloves, peppercorns, cardamom seeds and cinnamon stick in a dry frying pan and roast for a couple of minutes over a medium heat until warm to the touch and fragrant. Take off the heat and allow to cool and then grind to a fine powder in a spice grinder or pestle and mortar. Set aside.

Put the remaining curry paste ingredients into a blender or food processor and pour in the roasted spice powder. Blend to a smooth, thick paste, adding just enough water to do so. Some blenders will require more water for blending but try to keep it to a minimum, adding a spoonful at a time and remembering that the paste needs to be thick, not runny.

Add the oil to your slow cooker in the sauté/searing mode or to a frying pan over a medium–high heat. When the oil is bubbling hot, sear the meat in small batches until browned, then transfer to a plate. Set aside. Pour in the curry paste. Fry it for a couple of minutes, stirring regularly, until it is sizzling and fragrant. Add the beef, potatoes, red onion, coconut milk, sugar and tamarind concentrate and stir well to combine.

Now cook all these ingredients in your slow cooker, with the lid on, for 4 hours on the high setting or 6–8 hours on low. The curry is ready when the meat and potatoes are tender.

Add the roasted peanuts and a couple of tablespoons of fish sauce. Try it and add more fish sauce and/or salt to taste. Garnish with a few leaves of holy basil and serve.

*NOTE
Many Thai fish sauces contain gluten, but there are gluten-free brands available.

GF*

TOM KHA GAI
SERVES 4

Tom kha gai is one of the most popular Thai soups, together with tom yum gai, so I knew I needed to include both in the book. This recipe could not be easier! You just have to throw the ingredients in and let your slow cooker do its job.

PREP TIME: 10 MINS
COOKING TIME: HIGH 3
HRS, LOW 6 HRS

500g (16oz) chicken thighs
   or breasts
2 lemongrass stalks (white
   parts only with thick outer
   layers removed) bruised and
   cut into about 6 slices
3 kaffir lime leaves, stems
   removed, thinly sliced
1 thumb-sized piece of
   galangal, sliced into
   7 pieces and bruised
10 coriander (cilantro) stems,
   finely chopped
1 litre (4 cups) shop-bought or
   homemade chicken stock
   (page 117) or water
400ml (1¾ cups) thick
   coconut milk
2 tbsp palm sugar
8 shiitake or chestnut
   mushrooms, quartered
   or halved
70ml (¼ cup) Thai fish sauce*
2 tbsp Chinese crispy chilli oil
80ml (⅓ cup) lime juice,
   or to taste
3 spring onions (scallions),
   roughly chopped

Place all the ingredients up to and including the mushrooms in your slow cooker and stir well. Slow cook on the high setting, covered with the lid, for 3 hours on the high setting or 6 hours on low.

When the chicken is cooked through and the broth is already starting to taste amazing, remove the chicken and shred it by hand or using a couple of forks.

Return the chicken to the broth and add a couple of tablespoons of fish sauce. Try the broth and add more fish sauce to taste, if needed. I usually add about 5 tablespoons but you might want more or less. Stir in the Chinese crispy chilli oil, with as many of the crispy chillies as you like, and also add the lime juice to taste.

Serve hot, garnished with the chopped spring onions and more crispy chilli oil, if you like.

*NOTE

Some Thai fish sauces contain gluten, but there are gluten-free brands available.

TOM YUM GAI
SERVES 4–6

I use bone-in thighs for this recipe, as the bones help produce a stock with more depth of flavour, which really makes this soup, as tom yum gai doesn't contain coconut. You could add homemade chicken stock (page 117) instead of water and then you could use boneless thigh or breast meat.

**PREP TIME: 10 MINS
COOKING TIME: HIGH 3
HRS, LOW 6 HRS**

2 tbsp rapeseed (canola) oil
2 banana shallots, finely
    chopped
1 litre (4 cups) water or
    shop-bought or homemade
    chicken stock (page 117)
1 tbsp tamarind concentrate
1 tbsp Thai red curry paste
2 tsp palm or white sugar
    (optional and to taste)
1 lemongrass stalk, smashed
    and cut into about 5 pieces
8 kaffir lime leaves, stems
    removed and leaves
    thinly sliced
2.5cm (1in) piece of galangal,
    thinly sliced
3 garlic cloves, roughly chopped
700g (1lb 9oz) chicken thighs
    on the bone (seared in the
    hot oil (page 6) if you wish)
10 baby sweetcorn, cut into
    1cm (½in) rounds
8 mushrooms, quartered
2 medium tomatoes, quartered
1 tbsp Chinese crispy chilli oil
2–4 tbsp Thai fish sauce*
3 green bird's eye chillies,
    smashed and sliced
    lengthways
1 small handful of coriander
    (cilantro) leaves, roughly
    chopped
3 spring onions (scallions),
    roughly chopped
2 handfuls of bean sprouts
    (optional)
50g (2oz) Chinese cabbage,
    shredded (optional)
1 carrot, grated (optional)

Heat the oil in your slow cooker using the sauté/searing mode or in a pan on your stove over a medium–high heat. Add the shallots and fry for about 3 minutes, or until soft and translucent.

In your slow cooker, cook the fried shallots with all the ingredients up to and including the mushrooms, with the lid on, for 3 hours on the high setting or 6 hours on low until the chicken is tender and cooked through.

Remove the chicken thighs and shred the meat by hand or using a couple of forks. You can discard the bones and skin. Return the shredded chicken to the soup and add the quartered tomatoes, the crispy chilli oil, 2 tablespoons of fish sauce, the bird's eye chillies and the coriander. Stir it all in and taste some. You can add more fish sauce if you want a saltier flavour or add more of the spicy, sweet and sour ingredients to taste.

To finish, add the spring onions and any other vegetables you would like to add. In this recipe I added bean sprouts, cabbage and grated carrot at the end of cooking to let them heat through, but this is totally optional.

To serve, divide the soup between 4–6 bowls and enjoy.

*NOTE

Some Thai fish sauces contain gluten, but there are gluten-free brands available.

BEEF RENDANG
SERVES 4

Rendang curries are dry curries. The sauce literally clings to the meat. If the curry has more sauce in it, it's referred to as a gulai, which is also very tasty. Depending on how much moisture is released from your beef during cooking, you might end up with something closer to a gulai than a rendang and you might also prefer that. If needed, and you want a traditional rendang, you can always cook the curry down in your slow cooker using the sauté/searing mode or in a pan on your stove over a medium–high heat.

PREP TIME: 15 MINS
COOKING TIME: HIGH 4 HRS, LOW 6 HRS

70ml (¼ cup) coconut or rapeseed (canola) oil
5cm (2in) real cinnamon stick
2 star anise
4 cloves
4 cardamom pods, lightly bruised
2 lemongrass stalks, white parts only, thinly sliced
800g (1lb 12oz) stewing steak, cut into bite-sized pieces
300ml (1¼ cups) thick coconut milk
1½ tsp tamarind concentrate
6 tbsp toasted fresh or frozen grated coconut (kerisik)*
1 tsp palm sugar, or to taste
5 makrut lime leaves, stems removed and thinly sliced
Sea salt, to taste

FOR THE CURRY PASTE
6 shallots, roughly chopped
6 garlic cloves, smashed
2.5cm (1in) piece of galangal, roughly chopped
2 lime leaves, stemmed and roughly chopped
2 lemongrass stalks, white parts only, thinly sliced
12 dried red chillies, soaked in water for 20 minutes, then roughly chopped

TO GARNISH
2 red spur chillies, thinly sliced
3 spring onions (scallions), thinly sliced

Start by preparing the rendang paste. Place all the ingredients in a blender and blend to a paste. You can add a little water to assist with blending, if needed. Set aside until ready to use.

To make the curry, heat the oil in your slow cooker using the sauté/searing mode or in a pan over a medium–high heat. When visibly hot, stir in the whole spices and allow to infuse into the hot oil for about 30 seconds.

Stir in the prepared rendang paste and fry for a couple of minutes to cook out the rawness. Now add the thinly sliced lemongrass and the beef and stir well to combine. Fry for about 5 minutes to brown and then add the coconut milk, tamarind concentrate, 4 tablespoons of the toasted coconut, the sugar and lime leaves. Stir in all these ingredients.

Slow cook, with the lid on, on the high setting for 4 hours or low for 6 hours. The curry is ready when the meat is tender but you might want to cook it down some. This is optional as it will be delicious without doing so, but rendang curries are traditionally dry curries.

Season with salt to taste and serve garnished with the remaining toasted coconut and the sliced spur chillies and spring onions.

*NOTE
To toast the grated coconut, simply pour it into a pan and dry-fry over a medium–high heat until light golden brown. You can also purchase toasted grated coconut, which is called kerisik.

BABI KECAP
SERVES 4

Babi kecap is a sweet and sour pork belly dish from Indonesia. Normally, you would need to watch it closely but your slow cooker makes your job much easier and will give you excellent results. You want the pork belly to be melt-in-your-mouth tender so be sure to test it before serving. Just cook a little longer if needed but that probably won't be necessary.

PREP TIME: 10 MINS
COOKING TIME: HIGH 4
HRS, LOW 6 HRS

2 tbsp rapeseed (canola) oil
700g (1lb 9oz) pork belly, cut
   into 5cm (2in) chunks
2 makrut lime leaves, stems
   removed and thinly sliced
1 tbsp medium hot sauce
   (of your choice)
1 tsp palm or light brown sugar
6 tbsp kecap manis*
1 tbsp tamarind concentrate
1 tbsp lemon juice
White rice, to serve
2 red spur chillies, thinly sliced,
   to garnish

FOR THE SAMBAL PASTE
5 banana shallots
3 candlenuts or macadamia
   nuts
3 red finger chillies,
   roughly chopped
4 garlic cloves, peeled
   and smashed
5cm (2in) piece of ginger,
   roughly chopped
½ tsp ground turmeric

Place all the ingredients for the sambal paste in a food processor and blend to a smooth paste. You might need to add a little water to assist blending. Set aside.

Heat the oil in your slow cooker using the sauté/searing mode or in a frying pan over a medium–high heat. When the oil is visibly hot, add the pork belly pieces and brown the meat for about 5 minutes. Depending on the size of your pan, you might need to do this in two batches or it won't sear but rather stew in its own juices.

Add the prepared sambal paste to the pan with all the seared meat and stir well to combine. Continue cooking for another 3 minutes to cook out the rawness of the sambal. Stir in the makrut lime leaves, hot sauce, sugar, kecap manis and tamarind concentrate, cover with the lid and slow cook on the high setting for 4 hours or low for 6 hours. Once the pork is tender, add the lemon juice.

Babi kecap can be served as it is or you can reduce it down so that the sauce is thick enough to cling to the pork belly pieces. I usually do this, but it is really good just as it is from the slow cooker served over white rice and garnished with the sliced spur chillies.

*NOTE
Kecap manis is a thick and sweet soy sauce available online, at Asian grocers and some supermarkets.

THAI PORK BELLY STEW
SERVES 4

Pork belly is amazing cooked this way. I learned the original recipe while at a hotel in Phuket. This simplified version offers all the flavour and delicious texture, but you can literally place your prepared ingredients in your slow cooker and walk away for 4–6 hours. What you get in the end is one of the best Thai dishes I know.

PREP TIME: 10 MINS
COOKING TIME: HIGH 4 HRS, LOW 6 HRS

8 garlic cloves
10 long coriander (cilantro) stalks
1 generous tbsp black peppercorns
2 tbsp rapeseed (canola) oil
1kg (2lb 4oz) pork belly, cut into bite-sized chunks
5cm (2in) real cinnamon stick
2 star anise
2 tbsp palm sugar
3 tbsp light soy sauce*
2 tbsp dark soy sauce*
2 tbsp oyster sauce*
2 tbsp Chinese rice wine
6 tbsp finely chopped coriander (cilantro), to garnish

Put the garlic, coriander stalks and black peppercorns in a pestle and mortar and pound to a paste. Set aside.

Heat the oil in your slow cooker using the searing/sauté mode or in a pan over a medium–high heat. When it begins to glisten from the heat, add the pork belly cubes and brown on all sides. This should take about 5 minutes but you might need to do this in batches. Don't overcrowd your pan or the meat will stew rather than sear. Transfer the browned meat to a plate and set aside.

Add the cinnamon stick and star anise to the remaining oil in the pan and let the spices infuse into the oil for about 30 seconds. Return the meat to the pan and add the sugar, soy sauces and the oyster sauce. Stir well until the sugar dissolves and then add the Chinese rice wine, the prepared garlic, coriander and black pepper paste and 250ml (1 cup) of water and bring to a simmer.

Put the lid on your slow cooker and cook on the high setting for 4 hours or low for 6 hours, or until the pork belly is really tender.

When the pork is ready, taste and adjust the flavours as necessary, then stir in the chopped coriander before serving.

*NOTE
Many soy and oyster sauces contain gluten, but there are gluten-free brands available.

BEEF PHO

SERVES 4–6

There is some essential work you need to do to make a good pho stock, but after that it is really easy to produce a clear and delicious beef stock. You could substitute a low-sodium shop-bought beef stock for the water and bones for a pho that is similar – and good – but not quite the same. I find preparing the stock easier and faster in a pot on the stovetop so I don't do this in the slow cooker. If you have a larger slow cooker, you can double or even triple this recipe.

PREP TIME: 60 MINS
OR LESS
COOKING TIME: HIGH 4
HRS, LOW 8+ HRS

2 large onions, quartered
200g (7oz) root ginger, sliced thinly down the middle to give large, thin pieces of ginger
1.5kg (3lb 5oz) beef marrow bones, sliced into pieces to expose the marrow (optional – see intro; if not preparing the homemade stock, follow the recipe exactly but leave out the steps of cleaning and adding the bones)
8 star anise
5 cardamom pods, seeds only
5 cloves
2 x 5cm (2in) real cinnamon sticks
1 generous tsp palm sugar
700g (1lb 7oz) brisket or skirt steak
2 litres (8 cups) boiling water (or beef stock if not using the homemade stock)
3–5 tbsp fish sauce*

TO SERVE
200g (7oz) dried rice pho noodles, cooked per packet instructions
Generous portions of Thai sweet basil, coriander (cilantro) and bean sprouts
Green chillies, cut into rings
Lime wedges
Sriracha sauce (optional)

If you have a gas burner, place the onions and ginger right on the flame to char on all sides. Otherwise, spray a frying pan with a thin coating of cooking spray and char them in the pan. Set aside for later.

Place the bones in a pot and cover with water. Bring to the boil, then cook for 5 minutes, skimming off any foam that floats to the top. This will get you a beautifully clear stock. Then pour the water out of the pot into the sink and then rinse each bone under water, getting them as clean as you can. This also helps achieve a clear stock.

Place the clean bones in your slow cooker with the charred onions and ginger. Add the whole spices, sugar and meat. Cover with the boiling water (or stock), then cover with the lid and cook on the high setting for 4 hours or on low for 8 hours, until the meat is tender.

Transfer the meat to a plate and let it cool a little. Slice it thinly and keep refrigerated until ready to serve. You could let the other ingredients continue to slowly simmer on low for 24 hours or up to 48 hours for an even better broth.

Pour the stock through a fine sieve into a large bowl. I line my sieve with cheesecloth for an extra-clear broth but that is optional. You can serve your pho immediately or cover the stock and place it in the fridge along with the cooked meat. If doing this, finish off your pho within 2 days or freeze it all for up to 6 months.

To finish, pour the prepared stock back into the slow cooker on sear mode or into a pot. Bring to the boil, then reduce to a simmer. Add fish sauce to taste – I usually add about 5 tablespoons.

Place 4–6 large serving bowls on the table and add a good mound of cooked noodles to each one. Top the noodles with thinly sliced brisket or skirt steak, then pour the hot beef broth over them to fill the bowls. Everyone at the table can then top their pho with garnishes of their choice. How much of each garnish really is up to them. If you have any meat or broth left over, they freeze really well.

*NOTE
Some fish sauces contain gluten, but there are gluten-free brands available.

MALAYSIAN DEVIL CURRY
SERVES 4

Malaysian devil curry is a popular dish for the Christian community in Malaysia, where it is served at big events such as Christmas and is often a way to use up leftovers, such as sausages and roast potatoes from Christmas dinner. It's spicy, hence the name. In this recipe you use chicken thighs but if you have any leftovers you would like to mix in, go for it. If using leftover meat, heat it first until piping hot before adding it to the sauce.

**PREP TIME: 10 MINS
COOKING TIME: HIGH 3¼
HRS, LOW 6 HRS**

1kg (2lb 2oz) bone-in
   chicken thighs
2 tbsp light soy sauce*
   or tamari (GF)
3 tbsp white wine vinegar,
   plus extra, if needed
2 tbsp rapeseed (canola) oil
1 tbsp mustard seeds
4 whole green finger chillies
1 tsp cracked black pepper
2 tbsp unseasoned passata
Sea salt, to taste
Pinch of sugar (optional)

FOR THE CURRY PASTE
15 dried red chillies, soaked
   in water for 20 minutes
2 fresh red finger or spur
   chillies, roughly chopped
10 shallots, roughly chopped
5 candlenuts or 8 macadamia
   nuts
6 garlic cloves, roughly chopped
2 lemongrass stalks, thinly
   sliced
2.5cm (1in) piece of ginger,
   roughly chopped
2.5cm (1in) piece of galangal,
   roughly chopped
1 tsp ground turmeric

Marinate the chicken pieces in the soy sauce and vinegar while you prepare the rest of the ingredients. Set aside.

Place all the ingredients for the paste in a blender and mix until smooth, adding just enough water to blend. You only want to add about 300ml (1¼ cups) of water to this recipe altogether, so measure that quantity and use what you need to make the paste, then reserve the remaining water for later. Set the paste aside.

Now heat the oil in your slow cooker using the sauté/searing mode or in a large saucepan over a high heat. When the oil begins to shimmer, quickly sear the chicken in small batches, transferring to a plate as you go, and set aside. Add a drop more oil, if needed, then stir in the mustard seeds. When they begin to pop, stir in the whole chillies and cracked black pepper and continue cooking for about 30 seconds. Add the blended curry paste to the pan and heat through for 2 or 3 minutes, stirring continuously, until fragrant and the oil is starting to separate and rise to the top.

Add the passata and stir well to combine. Stir in the seared chicken pieces and any meat juices and add the remaining water. Bring to a simmer and then turn off the heat. Slow cook, covered with the lid, on the high setting for 3 hours or on low for 6 hours.

To finish, season with salt to taste. You can also add a little sugar if you prefer a sweeter flavour. I usually add a bit more vinegar, too.

*NOTE
Many soy sauces contain gluten, but there are gluten-free brands available.

KARI AYAM

SERVES 4

Kari Ayam is a Malaysian curry that's nice and spicy with an amazing flavour from lots of other ingredients. The broth is runnier and soupier than most curries. There is a heavy use of curry powder in kari ayam so be sure to use a good-quality one – not one that's been sitting at the back of your cupboard for months! Why not try making your own with my recipe on page 118?

PREP TIME: 15 MINS
COOKING TIME: HIGH 3¼
HRS, LOW 6 HRS

3 green cardamom pods
2 garlic cloves
5cm (2in) piece of root ginger
3 banana shallots
2 lemongrass stalks, tough outer
    parts removed
3 tbsp rapeseed (canola),
    coconut or peanut oil
5cm (2in) real cinnamon stick
2 star anise
20 fresh or frozen curry leaves
700g (1lb 9oz) chicken thighs
    and/or legs, skin optional (and
    seared (page 6) if you wish)
2 large potatoes, peeled and cut
    into bite-sized pieces
250ml (1 cup) thick coconut milk
½ tsp tamarind concentrate
70ml (¼ cup) shop-bought or
    homemade chicken stock
    (page 117) or water
Sea salt, to taste
3 tbsp finely chopped coriander
    (cilantro), to garnish
2 red spur chillies or spicier
    red bird's eye, thinly sliced,
    to garnish
Lemon wedges and rice, to serve

FOR THE AROMATIC PASTE

4 garlic cloves, smashed
2.5cm (1in) piece of root ginger,
    roughly chopped
4 banana shallots

FOR THE CHILLI PASTE

4 generous tbsp Curry powder
    (page 118) or shop-bought
    Malaysian curry powder
1 generous tbsp Kashmiri chilli
    powder, or to taste

Start by preparing the two pastes. To make the aromatic paste, place the garlic, ginger, shallots and 125ml (½ cup) of water in a blender and blend until smooth. Set aside. To make the chilli paste, pour the curry powder and chilli powder into bowl and pour in 125ml (½ cup) of water. Stir with a spoon until smooth, then set aside.

Now, for the curry, start by bruising the cardamom pods. Finely chop the garlic, then peel and julienne the ginger. Thinly slice the banana shallots, then lightly bruise the stalk of the lemongrass stalks.

Heat the oil in a large pan over a medium–high heat or using the sauté/sear setting of your slow cooker. When the oil begins to shimmer, add the cinnamon stick, star anise and bruised cardamom pods and stir for 30 seconds to infuse their flavours into the oil.

Now add the garlic, ginger and shallots and fry for another minute, then the add the curry leaves and lemongrass stalks and fry for another minute. Add the prepared aromatic paste and chilli paste and stir well to combine. Continue frying for about 3 minutes, at which time the sauce will have darkened a few shades.

Add the chicken and potatoes, stir well to coat with all the other ingredients and fry for a few minutes, or until the meat is turning white. Pour it all into your slow cooker and add the coconut milk, tamarind concentrate and the stock or water. Cover with the lid and slow cook on the high setting for 3 hours or low for 6 hours until the potatoes are tender and the chicken is cooked through.

Season with salt to taste and serve garnished with the chopped coriander and chillies. I like to serve this curry over rice with lemon wedges that can be squeezed over it all at the table to taste.

ASIAN PORK BONE BROTH

SERVES 4, OR MANY MORE

I have a bone broth like the one you'll use in this recipe in my slow cooker all the time. The longer it cooks, the better it gets and it's so nice to have on hand. Seriously... I cook this broth for about a week sometimes, straining and then adding new bones, aromatics and water every two days. Sometimes I make it with just chicken bones or a combination of pork and chicken. Once the broth is cooked to your liking, you are free to add your toppings of choice and enjoy. There's really no need to go out and spend over the odds for a soup like this when it is so easily prepared in your slow cooker. The toppings you add are up to you. Add fish sauce and sriracha to taste for a Thai-flavoured soup, for example. The toppings I suggest for this recipe are perfect because there aren't many additional cooking requirements, like steaming, needed.

PREP TIME: 10 MINS
COOKING TIME: 8 HRS+

2kg (4lb) meaty pork bones
    such as spare ribs or neck
1 onion, quartered
8 large garlic cloves,
    lightly smashed
2 thumb-sized pieces of ginger,
    sliced into a few pieces
5 spring onions (scallions),
    tied together

SUGGESTED ADDITIONS

1 serving of cooked ramen or
    rice noodles per person,
    cooked per package
    instructions
Soy sauce, to taste*
500g (1lb 4oz) minced
    (ground) pork, fried
    until cooked through
12 tbsp crispy fried onions,
    shop-bought or homemade
    (page 51)
½ green cabbage, thinly sliced
8 tbsp sambal oelek
12 tbsp spring onions (scallions),
    thinly sliced into rings
Hot chilli oil, to taste

Wash the pork bones and place them in your slow cooker. Add the onion, garlic, ginger and spring onions and top it all with water up to the maximum fill limit of your slow cooker. My slow cooker holds 8 litres (8.4 quarts) but a smaller slow cooker will work too. You just won't get as much! Cook on high for about an hour or until the broth begins to simmer. Then reduce the heat to low to cook for 8 hours or longer, being sure to skim any impurities that rise to the top during the first few hours.

Your bone broth can cook like this for up to 48 hours, and the longer you cook it, the better it will be. After 48 hours, carefully remove the bones and aromatic ingredients with a fine sieve, being careful not to move these ingredients around very much when doing so, so that you have a clearer broth. Use the broth in this soup or keep it cooking for even more flavour. If you want to cook the broth for longer, add fresh pork, the other half of the head of garlic, more ginger and spring onions and top it up with fresh water if you used some of the broth in the soup. Bring it to a simmer again on high and then reduce to low to continue cooking. You will need to skim off the impurities again after adding the pork.

To serve, put a portion of noodles in each of 4 bowls. Top the noodles with a couple of ladles of the broth and let everyone add what they want to it at the table.

*NOTES

Important! Although I do leave my stock simmering for up to a week at times, please google how to best keep it safe for consumption and free of harmful bacteria if you decide to do the same.

Many soy sauces contain gluten, but there are gluten-free brands available.

BASICS

Every cookbook needs a few basics and this book
is no exception. In addition to rice recipes that you
can use as a side or in Lamb dum biryani (page 51),
you will also find recipes for delicious spice
blends, curry pastes and stocks that you can use
in your curries, soups and stews to really take
them up a notch or two.

SLOW-COOKER RICE
SERVES 4–6

Cooking basmati or jasmine rice on your stove is easy and also faster than slow cooking it, but this is a great, simple recipe if you just want to get on with other things while your rice cooks. The recipe works for both basmati and jasmine rice – the only difference in the cooking method is that you don't need to soak jasmine rice before cooking; with basmati rice you do. For additional flavour, you could add whole spices like cinnamon, black peppercorns and cardamom pods just to name a few.

PREP TIME: 5 MINS
COOKING TIME: 2½ HRS

420g (2⅓ cups) basmati or
   jasmine rice
1 tbsp soft unsalted butter
1 litre (4 cups) boiling water
   from the kettle
1 tsp sea salt

In a mixing bowl, wash the rice in several changes of water. At first, the water will be milky from the starch on the rice but after about five changes of water it will be almost clear. If cooking basmati rice, soak the rice for about an hour in fresh water and then strain it. If using jasmine rice, you can go straight to cooking.

Rub the butter all over the bottom of your slow cooker pot and then add the rice, boiling water and salt. If you are not using a multi-cooker, which normally have tight screw-on lids, cover the slow cooker tightly with foil and then place the lid on top. Cook on the low setting for 2–2½ hours or until the rice has soaked up all the water. If you find that the rice is still a bit hard, you can add about 70ml (¼ cup) of boiling water and cook for another 30 minutes.

When the rice is cooked, transfer it to a bowl so that it doesn't continue to cook.

Carefully fluff up the rice with a fork or chop sticks. Do not stir too vigorously or the rice grains will split and become mushy.

If you have leftover rice, you can rinse it with cold water to cool it quickly and store it, covered, in your fridge for up to 4 days or freeze it for later. For food safety reasons, be sure that when reheating, it is piping hot before serving.

BOILED BASMATI RICE

SERVES 4

I included this easy boiled basmati rice here because if you're cooking a curry in your slow cooker, you might want to be able to whip up some rice to go on the side. You can easily up- or downscale this recipe as the water-to-rice ratio isn't important. You just need to ensure you have a large pot with enough water so that the grains of rice can float around freely as it simmers.

PREP TIME: 2 MINS,
PLUS SOAKING
COOKING TIME: 10 MINS

420g (2⅓ cups) basmati rice
Pinch of sea salt
A little butter

Put the uncooked rice in a large bowl and cover with cold water. Swirl the water around with your hands; it will become milky from the rice starch. Pour the water out and add fresh water and repeat until the water is almost clear – about five times should do the job. Leave the rice to soak in the last batch of fresh water for about 30 minutes, then drain.

Bring a large saucepan of water to the boil, then add the rice. Stir in the salt and butter, reduce the heat and simmer for 7–9 minutes. To check for doneness, take out a couple of grains and press them with your fingers. They should be soft but still have a bit of resistance to them.

Carefully pour the rice into a colander. If serving immediately, transfer to a serving dish and your job is done. If storing for later, rinse with cold water to cool it quickly, carefully stir through and place in an airtight container in the fridge for up to 4 days. For food safety reasons, be sure that when reheating, it is piping hot before serving.

FISH STOCK
MAKES 1 LITRE (4 CUPS)

If you're thinking about making one of the fish curries in this book – or any recipe that calls for fish stock – this straightforward recipe will provide much more depth of flavour than simply adding water. The recipe can easily be up- or downscaled depending on how much you require. The fish-to-water ratio is always 1:2, so if you're making a litre of fish stock, you need to use 500ml (2 cups) of fish pieces, such as the scraps you find at some fishmongers, bones or heads. Add more if you like and adjust the water as needed. Avoid using oily fish pieces, such as those you get from salmon and mackerel, and use fish or fish bones from bass, bream, cod, or crab or prawn shells etc.

PREP TIME: 5 MINS
COOKING TIME: LOW
6–8 HRS

500g (2 packed cups)
    fish pieces
1 onion, quartered
5 spring onions (scallions)
2 thumb-sized pieces of root
    ginger, cut into rings
4 garlic cloves
1 litre (4 cups) water

Place the fish pieces, onion, spring onions, ginger and garlic in your slow cooker and cover with the water. Although you can cover with the lid and cook this on the high setting for 3 hours, if time permits, I would recommend that you cook it for 6–8 hours on low.

Sieve through a fine strainer and discard the fish pieces. Pour the stock into a jar with a tight-fitting lid. This will keep for 4 days in the fridge. Although you can freeze it for up to 6 months, I don't recommend freezing fish stock as you will lose some flavour, so I suggest just making as much as you need for the recipe you are making. If freezing, be sure to date and label the container you freeze it in.

CHICKEN STOCK
MAKES 1 LITRE (4 CUPS)

Like the fish stock above, this is chicken stock in its simplest form. It offers a way of introducing more body to your curries rather than simply adding water. Most curries, soups and stews have enough flavoursome ingredients in them that you really don't need to put them in your stock too. That said, you could pimp up this stock for many different recipes if you want to. For example, for an Eastern-style stock, consider adding one onion, a carrot, some fresh coriander (cilantro) and aromatic ingredients like garlic, galangal, ginger and/or lemongrass. This recipe can easily be upscaled by adding more chicken bones or wings and water.

PREP TIME: 5 MINS
COOKING TIME: LOW
6–8 HRS

1 chicken carcass or the
    equivalent, broken
    into pieces
1 onion, quartered
5 spring onions (scallions)
2 thumb-sized pieces of root
    ginger, cut into rings
4 garlic cloves
1 litre (4 cups) water (approx.)

Place the chicken bones, onion, spring onions, ginger and garlic in your slow cooker and cover completely with the water. You can add more bones than called for in this recipe for a stronger flavour. Cover with the lid and cook on the low setting for 6–8 hours. You could speed up this process by cooking on high for 3 hours but I prefer slowly cooking the stock as long as I can. The stock will keep for about 4 days in an airtight container in your fridge and it also freezes well. If freezing, be sure to date and label the container/s and freeze for up to 6 months.

CURRY POWDER

MAKES 285G (2½ CUPS)

This curry powder is so much better than any you can purchase. The reason for this is that the whole spices in most commercial brands are not roasted before grinding.

PREP TIME: 8 MINS
COOKING TIME: 2 MINS

6 tbsp coriander seeds
6 tbsp cumin seeds
4 tbsp black peppercorns
2 tbsp fennel seeds
2 tbsp black mustard seeds
12cm (5in) real cinnamon stick
   or cassia bark
4 Indian bay leaves
   (cassia leaves)
3 tbsp fenugreek seeds
3 star anise
15 cardamom pods,
   lightly bruised
8 Kashmiri dried red chillies
   (optional)
2 tbsp ground turmeric
2 tbsp hot chilli powder
   (optional)
1 tsp garlic powder
2 tsp dried onion powder

Roast all the whole spices, including the dried chillies (if using), in a dry frying pan over a medium–high heat until warm to the touch and fragrant but not smoking. Be sure to move the spices around in the pan so that they roast evenly. Be careful not to burn them or they will become bitter and you will have to start again.

Tip the warm spices onto a plate and leave to cool, then grind to a fine powder in a spice grinder or pestle and mortar. Add the turmeric, chilli powder (if using), garlic powder and onion powder, and stir to combine.

Store in an airtight container in a cool, dark place and use within 2 months for optimal flavour.

NOTE
This makes about 20 generous tablespoons.

MIXED POWDER

MAKES 250G (2 CUPS)

Mixed powder is a special blend of spices used at curry houses around the UK. It's easy to prepare and it is usually made with shop-bought curry powder and garam masala. If you make your own using the recipes in this book, you will be taking your curry-house-style curries up a notch or two. This is a Madras style curry powder because of the dried chillies. You can leave them out or reduce the amount of dried chillies for a milder curry powder.

PREP TIME: 5 MINS

3 tbsp ground cumin
3 tbsp ground coriander
4 tbsp homemade Curry powder
   (above) or good quality shop-
   bought
3 tbsp paprika
3 tbsp ground turmeric
1 tbsp Garam masala (opposite)

Mix all the ingredients together, store in an airtight container in a cool, dark place, and use as needed. If you are using fresh, homemade garam masala and curry powder in your blend, your mixed powder should last for up to 2 months without losing much flavour.

NOTE
This makes about 17 generous tablespoons.

TANDOORI MASALA

MAKES 120G (1¼ CUPS)

All tandoori masalas are not equal. I have tried some brands that were simply made with ground cumin, ground coriander and citric acid along with red food colouring. With this recipe, you will be adding so much more to your curries and tandoori marinades and you will notice the difference!

PREP TIME: 8 MINS
COOKING TIME: 2 MINS

3 tbsp coriander seeds
3 tbsp cumin seeds
1 tbsp black mustard seeds
5cm (2in) real cinnamon stick
Small piece of mace
3 dried Indian bay leaves
   (cassia leaves)
1 tbsp ground ginger
2 tbsp garlic powder
2 tbsp dried onion powder
2 tbsp amchoor (dried
   mango powder)
1 tbsp (or more) red food
   colouring powder (optional)

Roast the whole spices in a dry frying pan over a medium–high heat until warm to the touch and fragrant, moving them around in the pan as they roast and being careful not to burn them. If they begin to smoke, take them off the heat. Tip onto a plate to cool.

Grind to a fine powder in a spice grinder or pestle and mortar, then tip into a bowl. Stir in the ground ginger, garlic powder, onion powder and amchoor. Stir in the red food colouring powder (if using). The masala will not look overly red like the commercial brands. Store in an airtight container in a cool, dark place and use as required, within 2 months for optimal flavour.

GARAM MASALA

MAKES 170G (1½ CUPS)

Garam masala is used in almost every Indian recipe. There are thousands of recipes for it but they all consist of warming spices such as cumin, coriander and cinnamon – so no chillies or chilli powder, as that would be a curry powder. I like to make my own, but you can find good-quality mixtures in Asian stores.

PREP TIME: 8 MINS
COOKING TIME: 2 MINS

6 tbsp coriander seeds
6 tbsp cumin seeds
5 tsp black peppercorns
4 tbsp fennel seeds
3 tsp cloves
7.5cm (3in) real cinnamon stick
5 dried Indian bay leaves
   (cassia leaves)
20 green cardamom pods,
   lightly bruised
2 large pieces of mace

Roast all the spices in a dry frying pan over a medium–high heat until warm to the touch and fragrant, moving them around in the pan as they roast and being careful not to burn them. If they begin to smoke, take them off the heat immediately.

Tip the warm spices onto a plate and leave to cool, then grind to a fine powder in a spice grinder or pestle and mortar.

Store in an airtight container in a cool, dark place and use within 2 months for optimal flavour.

GARLIC AND GINGER PASTE

MAKES ABOUT 250G (1 CUP)

I always make my own garlic and ginger paste. Sometimes I add chillies to taste to make garlic, ginger and chilli paste. The process is easy and the results are so much better than the pastes you purchase in jars. If you want to purchase garlic and ginger paste, I recommend looking for frozen garlic and ginger cubes, which can be found at most Indian grocers.

PREP TIME: 10 MINS

150g (5½oz) garlic, roughly chopped
150g (5½oz) root ginger, peeled and roughly chopped

Place the garlic and ginger in a food processor or pestle and mortar and blend with just enough water to make a smooth paste. Some chefs finely chop their garlic and ginger instead, which is a good alternative to making a paste. Store in an airtight container in the fridge for up to 3 days and use as needed. If you're planning a curry party, go ahead and get this job ticked off early. The paste can turn a bit blue or green while in the fridge. This is natural and it is not off.

I often make larger batches and freeze it in ice cube trays. Once frozen, the cubes can be transferred to airtight plastic bags in the freezer, ready for when you get that curry craving. Be sure to let them defrost a little first.

EASY TANDOORI MARINADE

SERVES 4

I have featured many tandoori marinades in my previous cookbooks and you could use any of them to marinate meat, paneer and vegetables for the recipes in this book. On pages 122 through 124, I have given recipes to make your own spice pastes. All of these will work as a marinade, either as they are or whisked with yoghurt if you want to marinate for longer than 4 hours. You could of course use shop-bought pastes but the homemade versions are far better!

PREP TIME: 5 MINS

800g (1lb 12 oz) protein of choice or vegetables
3–4 tbsp curry paste of choice
4 tbsp Greek yoghurt (optional)

You need to add the yoghurt if you are marinating meat for longer than 4 hours. The yoghurt also adds flavour so you can add it anyway if you like. Mix well to combine and allow your meat, paneer or vegetables to marinate until needed. Scrape off most of the marinade before frying for a curry and carry on with the recipe. This is an alternative to cooking these ingredients simply sprinkled with salt and will add another layer of flavour.

CURRY PASTES

I am often asked by people who are new to cooking curries, why not just use a shop-bought curry paste? Well, the answer is that you have a lot more control over the flavour of the curry when you get to know your spices and can add them individually to taste. Using a curry paste can be a bit of a cheat and they are also why so many curry houses use shop-bought pastes. The following curry pastes are no cheats, though. You will be roasting and grinding the spices to perfection before making them into a paste offering delicious flavour and convenience.

I have been wanting to share these recipes with you for a while and this book seemed like the perfect place to do so. Slow cooking is great for replicating the slowly cooked curries, stews and soups from around the Indian subcontinent and South East Asia. For many people, slow cooking is also done for convenience, and these pastes will make throwing a good curry together quickly to slow cook that much easier.

All the spice pastes take 15 minutes to prep and 2 minutes of cooking. All of them will last for 3 months in the fridge.

THE SPICE PASTES

To develop the spice paste recipes, I tried and looked at the ingredients of several well-known brands. I wanted to make them similar but better. I find commercial pastes a bit boring and samey because the spices do not taste like they have been roasted and most have a bit too much acid for my liking.

The pastes, both shop-bought and homemade, are there for convenience. You might notice that some of the following spice pastes call for different ingredients than I use in the recipes in the book. My jalfrezi paste recipe, for example, calls for a few different ingredients than are listed in the jalfrezi curry recipe. There is more than one way to make a jalfrezi after all, so you could use a paste or make the jalfrezi curry recipe as written and you will still end up with a jalfrezi!

When adding the pastes to a curry, you are only using them as a substitute for the ground spices. Everything else in the recipe remains the same. For example, if a recipe calls for ground almonds or garlic and ginger paste, you still add them.

HOW MUCH PASTE SHOULD YOU USE?

In each recipe where I often use pastes, I suggest an amount of paste to use, usually 3–4 generous tablespoons, but that's just a suggestion. Add them to taste. The recipes make about 12 heaped tablespoons. You might also like to add a tablespoon of paste to any curry as a bit of a flavour booster. Many curry-house chefs add their spices individually and then top up a curry at the end with a commercial paste. If it sounds good, do it.

ADDING SALT

Whether you include salt is very much up to you. I usually leave it out when making the paste, then season to taste when I am actually cooking the curry.

OTHER WAYS TO USE THESE PASTES…

Just because you make a rogan josh paste or a tikka masala paste, it doesn't mean you have to only use them in those curries. You will find that the individual spice blends are quite similar. You can mix them together to come up with a curry of your own. You could also try using a tikka masala or rogan josh paste in a Madras curry instead of Madras paste. Feel free to experiment and adjust the flavours accordingly with individual spices. You really can't go wrong.

TIKKA MASALA PASTE

MAKES 250ML (1 CUP)

To use this in a chicken tikka masala, replace the spices in the recipe with 3–4 tablespoons of this paste. It can also be whisked to taste into yogurt for an easy raita or used to marinate meat and vegetables. To do this, coat the meat or vegetables, then stir in a few tablespoons of yogurt.

4 tbsp cumin seeds
4 tbsp coriander seeds
1 tbsp black peppercorns
1 tbsp paprika
1 tbsp Kashmiri chilli powder,
    or to taste, or more paprika
1 tsp amchoor (dried
    mango powder)
½ tsp ground turmeric
½ tsp ground ginger
1 tsp ground garlic
1 tbsp kasoori methi (dried
    fenugreek leaves)
1 tbsp dried coriander (cilantro)
1 tbsp tamarind concentrate
150ml (⅔ cup) vegetable oil
    (plus more if required)
70ml (¼ cup) distilled vinegar
    or white wine vinegar
Sea salt, to taste (optional)

Heat a frying pan over a medium–high heat. Pour the whole spices into the pan and roast until warm to the touch and fragrant but don't let them smoke. Remove the spices from the heat to cool on a plate and then place the spices in a spice grinder or pestle and mortar and blend to a fine powder. Stir in the paprika, chilli powder, amchoor, turmeric, ground ginger, ground garlic, kasoori methi and coriander leaves.

In a frying pan, mix this powder with the tamarind concentrate and about 100ml (⅓ cup) of water and stir into a paste over a medium heat. Pour the oil into the pan and turn the burner up to medium–high. Stir continuously until the spices begin to sizzle a bit and the oil all rises to the top – 30 seconds to a minute should be enough, as you have already roasted the spices.

Turn off the heat, add the vinegar and stir it all up nicely. Season with salt, if using. Spoon the spice mixture into a very clean preserves jar with an airtight lid.

ROGAN JOSH PASTE

MAKES 250ML (1 CUP)

Great in a rogan josh curry or any curry for that matter – the great thing about all these curry pastes is that they are so versatile.

4 tbsp coriander seeds
2 tbsp fennel seeds
4 tbsp cumin seeds
1 tbsp black peppercorns
Seeds from 4 green
    cardamom pods
4 cloves
3 tbsp paprika
1 tsp amchoor (dried mango
    powder)
½ tsp ground turmeric
½ tsp ground ginger
1 tsp garlic powder
1 tsp sea salt, to taste (optional)
2 tsp tamarind concentrate
125ml (½ cup) rapeseed
    (canola) oil
70ml (¼ cup) white wine vinegar

Heat a frying pan over a medium–high heat. Pour the whole spices into the pan and roast until warm to the touch and fragrant but don't let them smoke. Remove the spices from the heat to cool on a plate and then place the spices in a spice grinder or pestle and mortar and blend to a fine powder. Stir in the paprika, amchoor, ground turmeric, ginger, garlic powder and salt, if using

In a frying pan, mix this powder with the tanarind concentrate and about 125ml (½ cup) of water and stir into a paste. Pour the oil into the pan and put over a medium–high heat. Stir continuously until the spices begin to sizzle a bit and the oil all rises to the top – 30 seconds to a minute should be enough, as you have already roasted the spices.

Turn off the heat, add the vinegar and stir it all up nicely. Spoon the spice mixture into a very clean preserves jar with an airtight lid.

KASHMIRI PASTE
MAKES ABOUT 250ML (1 CUP)

This is a good all-rounder that can be added to most curries, including a mild pasanda or korma, for a bit more kick. Add it one tablespoon at a time at the end of cooking to taste.

4 tbsp coriander seeds
2 tbsp fennel seeds
4 tbsp cumin seeds
1 tbsp black peppercorns
10 dried Kashmiri red chillies, or to taste
3cm (1¼in) real cinnamon stick
1 tbsp paprika
1 tsp amchoor (dried mango powder)
1 tsp garlic powder
½ tsp ground ginger
½ tsp ground turmeric
125ml (½ cup) rapeseed (canola) oil
70ml (¼ cup) white wine vinegar
Sea salt, to taste (optional)

Heat a frying pan over a medium–high heat. Pour the whole spices into the pan and roast until warm to the touch and fragrant but don't let them smoke. Remove the spices from the heat and leave to cool on a plate, then place the spices in a spice grinder or pestle and mortar and blend to a fine powder. Stir in the paprika, amchoor, garlic powder, ginger and ground turmeric

In a frying pan, mix this powder with about 100ml (scant 1 cup) of water and stir into a paste. Pour the oil into the pan, and put over a medium–high heat. Stir continuously until the spices begin to sizzle a bit and the oil all rises to the top – 30 seconds to a minute should be enough, as you have already roasted the spices. Season with salt, if using.

Turn off the heat, add the vinegar and stir it all up nicely. Spoon the spice mixture into a very clean preserves jar with an airtight lid.

VINDALOO PASTE
MAKES 250ML (1 CUP)

When I developed this curry paste I was trying to copy a commercial brand but make it better. I was surprised at how mild the commercial vindaloo paste was but decided to keep the spice level similar. It's all about the chilli powder – add more if you want to take that zing to a zap!

4 tbsp coriander seeds
4 tbsp cumin seeds
1 tbsp black peppercorns
1 tsp black mustard seeds
Seeds from 4 green cardamom pods
4 cloves
5cm (2in) real cinnamon stick
1 tbsp fenugreek seeds
1 tbsp paprika
2 tbsp Kashmiri chilli powder
1 tsp amchoor (dried mango powder)
½ tsp ground turmeric
1 tsp garlic powder
1 tsp sea salt, to taste
1 tsp tamarind concentrate
125ml (½ cup) rapeseed (canola) oil
70ml (¼ cup) white wine vinegar

Heat a frying pan over a medium–high heat. Pour the whole spices into the pan and roast until warm to the touch and fragrant but don't let them smoke. Remove the spices from the heat to cool on a plate.

Place the spices in a spice grinder or pestle and mortar and blend to a fine powder. Stir in the paprika, chilli powder, amchoor, turmeric, garlic powder and salt, if using.

In a frying pan, mix this powder with the tamarind concentrate and about 125ml (½ cup) of water and stir into a paste. Pour the oil into the pan and put the pan over a medium–high heat. Stir continuously until the spices begin to sizzle a bit and the oil all rises to the top – 30 seconds to a minute should be enough, as you have already roasted the spices.

Turn off the heat, add the vinegar and stir it all up nicely. Spoon the spice mixture into a very clean preserves jar with an airtight lid.

MADRAS PASTE
MAKES 250ML (1 CUP)

Like the Vindaloo paste (page 123), this Madras curry paste is meant to be a bit spicy. Try it though – you might want to add more or less chilli powder.

4 tbsp coriander seeds
4 tbsp cumin seeds
1 tbsp black peppercorns
1 tsp black mustard seeds
Seeds from 4 green
   cardamom pods
4 cloves
1 tbsp fenugreek seeds
2 tbsp paprika
2–3 tbsp Kashmiri chilli powder
1 tsp amchoor (dried
   mango powder)
½ tsp ground turmeric
½ tsp ground ginger
1 tsp garlic powder
1 tsp sea salt, to taste (optional)
1 tsp tamarind concentrate
125ml (½ cup) rapeseed
   (canola) oil
3 tbsp white wine vinegar

Heat a frying pan over a medium–high heat. Pour the whole spices into the pan and roast until warm to the touch and fragrant but don't let them smoke. Remove the spices from the heat to cool on a plate and then place the spices in a spice grinder or pestle and mortar and blend to a fine powder. Stir in the paprika, chilli powder, amchoor, ground turmeric, ground ginger, garlic powder and salt, if using.

In a frying pan, mix this powder with the tamarind concentrate and about 125ml (½ cup) of water and stir into a paste. Pour the oil into the pan and turn your burner on to medium–high. Stir continuously until the spices begin to sizzle a bit and the oil all rises to the top – 30 seconds to a minute should be enough, as you have already roasted the spices.

Turn off the heat, add the vinegar and stir it all up nicely. Spoon the spice mixture into a very clean preserves jar with an airtight lid.

JALFREZI PASTE
MAKES 250ML (1 CUP)

This paste will make a delicious jalfrezi! You might like to try it in another curry too. Try it instead of the usual paste in a chicken tikka masala. If you like a spicy curry, you'll love it!

4 tbsp coriander seeds
4 tbsp cumin seeds
2 tbsp fennel seeds
1 tbsp black peppercorns
2 tbsp desiccated (dried
   shredded) coconut
2 tbsp paprika
1 tbsp Kashmiri chilli powder
1 tsp amchoor (dried
   mango powder)
½ tsp ground turmeric
1 tsp garlic powder
1 tsp sea salt, to taste (optional)
2 tsp tamarind concentrate
125ml (½ cup) rapeseed
   (canola) oil
70ml (¼ cup) white wine vinegar

Heat a frying pan over a medium–high heat. Pour the whole spices into the pan and roast until warm to the touch and fragrant but don't let them smoke. Remove the spices from the heat to cool on a plate. Now toast the desiccated coconut in the pan for a couple of minutes until it turns a light golden brown. Transfer to the plate with the roasted spices and allow it all to cool a little.

Place the spices and coconut in a spice grinder or pestle and mortar and blend to a fine powder. Stir in the paprika, Kashmiri chilli powder, amchoor, turmeric, garlic powder and salt, if using.

In a frying pan, mix the powder with the tamarind concentrate and about 125ml (½ cup) of water and stir into a paste. Pour the oil into the pan and place over a medium–high heat. Stir continuously until the spices begin to sizzle a bit and the oil all rises to the top – 30 seconds to a minute should be enough.

Turn off the heat, add the vinegar and stir it all up nicely. Spoon the spice mixture into a very clean preserves jar with an airtight lid.

INDEX

Managing Director: Sarah Lavelle
Editor: Sofie Shearman
Designer: Katy Everett
Cover Design: Smith & Gilmour
Photographer: Kris Kirkham
Photography Assistants: Phoebe Pearson,
Rob Perry and Zoe Warde-Aladam
Food Stylist: Rosie Reynolds
Food Stylist Assistants: Jessica Geddes
Props Stylist: Faye Wears
Head of Production: Stephen Lang
Production Manager: Sabeena Atchia

Colour reproduction by p2d
Printed in China by C&C Offset Printing Co., Ltd.

The authorised representative in the EEA is Penguin
Random House Ireland, Morrison Chambers,
32 Nassau Street, Dublin D02 YH68.

Penguin Random House is committed to a sustainable
future for our business, our readers and our planet.
This book is made from Forest Stewardship Council®
certified paper.

Quadrille, Penguin Random House UK, One Embassy
Gardens, 8 Viaduct Gardens, London SW11 7BW
Quadrille Publishing Limited is part of the Penguin
Random House group of companies whose addresses
can be found at global.penguinrandomhouse.com

Penguin
Random House
UK

Published by Quadrille in 2026
www.penguin.co.uk
A CIP catalogue record for this book is available
from the British Library
ISBN 978 183 783 499 0
10 9 8 7 6 5 4 3 2 1

MIX
Paper | Supporting
responsible forestry
FSC® C018179

ACKNOWLEDGEMENTS

It was a pleasure to once again work with everyone
at Quadrille to produce this book. Thank you to
Sarah Lavelle for commissioning the project and to
my editors, Wendy Hobson and Sofie Shearman,
for all their help with my words and for bringing it
all together.

Thanks to Kris Kirkham, who has worked
with me on every cookbook I've written, and
food stylist Rosie Reynolds for bringing my recipes
to life in a way that only they can. Thank you also
to Kris's assistants, Phoebe Pearson, Rob Perry and
Zoe Warde-Aladam and food stylist assistant Jess
Geddes. We could not have done it without them!

Thank you to props stylist Faye Wears, who
sourced the props and dishes. They were perfect!

A big thank you goes out to the moderators of
my Facebook group: Jon Monday, Steven Lumsden,
Tim Martin, Karen Bolan, Claire Rees, Anne-Marie
Goodfellow, James Vaisey. Your help and support is
so much appreciated.

Thank you to my agent, Clare Hulton, for all her
support and for once again making things happen.

I could not have written this book without
my wife Caroline's support. She helped cook every
recipe to ensure that the recipes worked and tasted
as they should.

I would also like to thank my son Joe Toombs
and his fiancé, Shannon Ellerton, for their help
with the recipes. They cooked and tested most,
if not all, of these recipes and filmed many of them
being made for my blog and social media. Their
feedback and help perfecting these recipes for the
home cook has been invaluable. They read and
prepared each recipe as written, sometimes
catching problems I didn't want going in a printed
book. Thank you!

One last big thank you, and that goes out to you
for picking up this book. I appreciate it so much
and hope you enjoy the book and recipes as much
as I enjoyed putting this collection together.